P9-CQC-671

*Able*MUSE
A REVIEW OF POETRY, PROSE & ART

NUMBER 21

Summer 2016

www.ablemuse.com

Able Muse Press
publishing the new, the established

Now available from Able Muse Press:

Able Muse Anthology
Edited by Alexander Pepple
Foreword by Timothy Steele

978-0-9865338-0-8 • $16.95

With R.S. Gwynn, Rhina P. Espaillat, Rachel Hadas, Mark Jarman, Timothy Murphy, Dick Davis, A.E. Stallings, Alan Sullivan, Deborah Warren, Diane Thiel, Leslie Monsour, Kevin Durkin, Turner Cassity, Kim Bridgford, Richard Moore and others.

. . . Here's a generous serving of the cream of Able Muse including not only formal verse but nonmetrical work that also displays careful craft, memorable fiction (seven remarkable stories), striking artwork and photography, and incisive prose. — X.J. Kennedy

Able Muse – Print Edition, No. 18
INCLUDES THE 2014 WRITE PRIZE WINNERS

WINTER 2014
WITH

POETRY, FICTION, BOOK REVIEWS, INTERVIEWS & ESSAYS from POEMS, FICTION, BOOK REVIEWS, INTERVIEWS & ESSAYS from gustavo thomas • david mason • haley leithauser • r.s. gwynn • kathrine coles • tamas dobozy • barbara haas • hollis seamon • derek furr • marilyn l. taylor • and others

ISBN 978-1-927409-47-3

Subscribe to: *Able Muse (Print Ed.)*

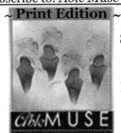

~ **Print Edition** ~

Semiannual review of poetry, prose & art

Able Muse (Print Edition) continues the excellence in poetry, art, fiction, essays, interviews and book reviews showcased all these years in the online edition. Subscribe at *www.ablemusepress.com*

For complete details, visit: **www.AbleMusePress.com**

visit
Able Muse

online for more than a decade of archives, plus web-only features not available in the Print Edition at:

www.ablemuse.com

Able Muse is not just another poetry site. It is one of the best sites on the Internet.
—Heather O'Neil, *Suite101.com*

A forum of Able Muse Review

Able Muse's premier online forums and workshops for metrical and non-metrical poetry, fiction, translations, art, nonfiction and discussions at:

http://eratosphere.ablemuse.com

Able Muse and its extraordinary companion website, the *Eratosphere*, have created a huge and influential virtual literary community. —Dana Gioia

Able Muse

www.ablemuse.com

Editor	Alexander Pepple
Assistant Poetry Editors	Nicole Caruso Garcia, Stephen Kampa, Richard Meyer, Callie Siskel
Nonfiction Editors	Robert B. Shaw, N.S. Thompson
Fiction Editor	Karen Kevorkian
Assistant Fiction Editors	Jonathan Danielson, Janice D. Soderling, Rob Wright
Editorial Board	Rachel Hadas, X.J. Kennedy, A.E. Stallings, Timothy Steele, Deborah Warren

Able Muse is published semiannually. Subscription rates—for individuals: $28.00 per year; libraries and institutions: $38 per year; single and previous issues: $19.95 + $3 S&H.
International subscription rates: $35 per year; single and previous issues: $19.95 + $5 S&H.
Subscribe online at www.ablemusepress.com or send a check payable to *Able Muse Review* to the snail mail address indicated below. (USD throughout. Online payment with WePay/credit card.)

We read year-round and welcome previously unpublished manuscripts only. No simultaneous submissions. Online or email submissions ONLY. Submission guidelines available at:
www.ablemuse.com/submit

Queries and other correspondence should be emailed to: editor@ablemuse.com
For paper correspondence, be sure to include a self-addressed, stamped envelope:

Attn: Alexander Pepple, Editor
Able Muse Review
467 Saratoga Avenue #602
San Jose, CA 95129

Library of Congress Control Number: 2016944441

ISBN 978-1-927409-78-7 (paperback) / ISBN 978-1-927409-79-4 (digital)

ISSN 2168-0426

Cover image: "Thirst" by Elijah Fayerman

Cover & book design by Alexander Pepple

www.ablemuse.com
editor@ablemuse.com

Printed in the United States of America
Published in 2016 by Able Muse Press: www.ablemusepress.com

Alexander Pepple

Editorial

Y ES, WE RARELY DO THEME ISSUES, but read through this one, and you might well discern a summer theme . . . or you might as readily glean a different theme as you take in the poetry, fiction, essays, book reviews, art and photography presented here, which include new poetry from our featured poet Amanda Jernigan, her interview with Ange Mlinko, and the wonderful nature photography of featured artist Andy Biggs.

Inside, you'll find new talk about Byron, an exposition on the architecture and history of the Resurrection Cathedral on Spilled Blood in Saint Petersburg, a polar and safari photographic showcase, musing on the contrapuntal bliss and vacillations of J.S. Bach's inventions, the storied lives of Stieglitz and O'Keeffe reimagined, and so much more.

Congratulations to Martin McGovern, 2016 finalist in the Colorado Book Award for *Bad Fame* (Able Muse Press, 2015). And welcome to our new assistant poetry editor Nicole Caruso Garcia, who replaces the departing Richard Meyer, with our thanks to both.

I hope you enjoy this issue of *Able Muse,* print edition, as much as we've enjoyed bringing it to you.

The very best,

Alexander Pepple
—Editor

Colorado Book Award
2016 Finalist

New Mexico-Arizona Book Award
2015 Finalist

Bad Fame
poems by **Martin McGovern**
978-1-927409-50-3 | Paperback

"Martin McGovern's long-awaited, well-constructed first book gives itself away slowly, artfully. It is carefully considered, quietly passionate, and deeply humane."
—Edward Hirsch

". . . the sentences, like the centuries, are treated pitilessly, as you can hear, yet there is what the poet calls 'the shimmer of a teen movie' throughout. Resilient art, and no loitering."
—Richard Howard

Cup
poems by **Jeredith Merrin**
SPECIAL HONOREE – 2013 ABLE MUSE BOOK AWARD

978-1-927409-34-3 | Paperback

"In these forthright and moving poems written in restrained, disciplined stanzas, the stories are told of how we each, 'trying to make it better,/ whatever . . . it is,' have to find our own cup, and find it acceptable."
— David Ferry

"In *Cup* we meet a poet of rare power and unique originality, unafraid of feeling, able to take on matters of the deepest consequence." — X.J. Kennedy

BOOKS

FROM

ABLE MUSE PRESS

NEW & RECENT RELEASES

EMILY LEITHAUSER: *The Borrowed World – Poems*
~ WINNER, 2016 ABLE MUSE BOOK AWARD ~

ELISE HEMPEL: *Second Rain – Poems*

CARRIE SHIPERS: *Cause for Concern – Poems*
~ WINNER, 2015 ABLE MUSE BOOK AWARD ~

GAIL WHITE: *Asperity Street – Poems*
~ SPECIAL HONOREE, 2014 ABLE MUSE BOOK AWARD ~

MELISSA BALMAIN: *Walking in on People – Poems*
~ WINNER, 2013 ABLE MUSE BOOK AWARD ~

JEREDITH MERRIN: *Cup – Poems*
~ SPECIAL HONOREE, 2013 ABLE MUSE BOOK AWARD ~

CHELSEA WOODARD: *Vellum – Poems*

D.R. GOODMAN: *Greed: A Confession – Poems*

RICHARD NEWMAN: *All the Wasted Beauty of the World – Poems*

ELLEN KAUFMAN: *House Music – Poems*

BARBARA ELLEN SORENSEN: *Compositions of the Dead Playing Flutes – Poems*

FRANK OSEN: *Virtue, Big as Sin – Poems*
~ WINNER, 2012 ABLE MUSE BOOK AWARD ~

JAMES POLLOCK: *Sailing to Babylon – Poems*

MATTHEW BUCKLEY SMITH: *Dirge for an Imaginary World – Poems*
~ WINNER, 2011 ABLE MUSE BOOK AWARD ~

APRIL LINDNER: *This Bed Our Bodies Shaped – Poems*

RICHARD WAKEFIELD: *A Vertical Mile – Poems*

JOHN RIDLAND: *Sir Gawain and the Green Knight – A New Modern English Verse Translation*

ALFRED NICOL: *Animal Psalms – Poems*

WILLIAM BAER: *Times Square and Other Stories*

JAN D. HODGE: *Taking Shape – Carmina Figurata*

HOLLIS SEAMON: *Corporeality – Stories*

WENDY VIDELOCK: *Slingshots and Love Plums – Poems*

MARTIN McGOVERN: *Bad Fame – Poems*

WILLIAM CONELLY: *Uncontested Grounds – Poems*

JOHN PHILIP DRURY: *Sea Level Rising – Poems*

CAROL LIGHT: *Heaven from Steam – Poems*

STEPHEN SCAER: *Pumpkin Chucking – Poems*

MARYANN CORBETT: *Credo for the Checkout Line in Winter – Poems*

WENDY VIDELOCK: *The Dark Gnu and Other Poems*

BEN BERMAN: *Strange Borderlands – Poems*

CATHERINE CHANDLER: *Lines of Flight – Poems*

MARGARET ANN GRIFFITHS: *Grasshopper: The Poetry of M A Griffiths*

WENDY VIDELOCK: *Nevertheless – Poems*

AARON POOCHIGIAN: *The Cosmic Purr – Poems*

MICHAEL CANTOR: *Life in the Second Circle – Poems*

LATEST ABLE MUSE PRESS CATALOG

Free Download at: **www.ablemusepress.com/catalog**

NEW FROM

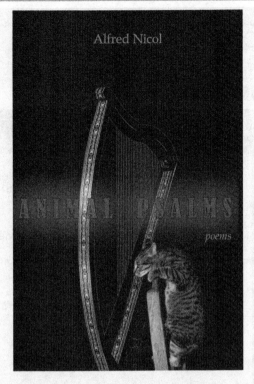

Animal Psalms
poems by Alfred Nicol
978-1-927409-69-5 | Paperback

"Dear reader, I've fallen in love with this book, and that will happen to you too . . . Read all the rest, these poems by Alfred Nicol which have our numbers, and have his own too . . . It's impossible not to fall in love."
—David Ferry

". . . Poise and wit prevail in these psalms; they give us both despair inflected by light and illumination held fast by darkness."
—Erica Funkhouser

". . . Don't be surprised if—after reading these poems—you find them turning back to their true subject, dear reader, which turns out to be none other than you."
—Paul Mariani

Second Rain
poems by **Elise Hempel**
978-1-927409-73-2 | Paperback

"The apparently domestic poems in Second Rain . . . deliver enough controlled intensity 'to shake the trees all down.'"
—Rachel Hadas

". . . From the opening title poem on, this is a book about the often ignored, simple gifts that come to us."
—Bruce Guernsey (from the foreword)

". . . Like the flock of geese described in one poem here, Hempel's collection succeeds in many 'different keys.'"
—James Scruton

". . . each piece in Second Rain 'briefly blesses you.'"
—Edward Byrne

Details at

ABLE MUSE PRESS

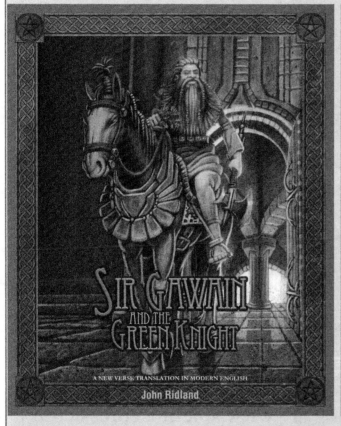

Sir Gawain and the Green Knight
a new Modern English verse translation
by John Ridland

PRAISE FOR RIDLAND'S TRANSLATION

★ ★ ★ ★ ★

John Ridland has given Sir Gawain and the Green Knight *a fresh lease on life.*
— X.J. Kennedy

Ridland gives the poem a long, loose line that sings in the lyrical passages, creeps in the spooky ones, and cavorts in the comic ones. Just as important, the densely mythic ethos, fully intact, enriches every word.
— Richard Wakefield

Panoramas of banqueting and hunting, closely observed rituals of dressing, arming, and game preparation, and rich descriptions of landscape and weather—Ridland's translation presents these in all their delightful, over-the-top particularity.
— Maryann Corbett (from the foreword)

. . . like all enchantments, it shifts and assumes different forms to different eyes. But I do guarantee surprises, and inexhaustible delight.
— Rhina P. Espaillat

124 pages
ISBN 978-1-927409-56-5 (paperback); ISBN 978-1-927409-58-9 (hardcover)

www.AbleMusePress.com

Able Muse – Print Edition, No. 20

INCLUDES THE 2015 WRITE PRIZE WINNERS

WINTER 2015

WITH

POETRY, FICTION, BOOK REVIEWS, INTERVIEWS & ESSAYS from léon leijdekkers ▪ amit majmudar ▪ x.j. kennedy ▪ wendy videlock ▪ stephen kampa ▪ kim bridgford ▪ n.s. thompson ▪ lynda sexson ▪ robert b. shaw ▪ moira egan ▪ jennifer reeser ▪ and others

ISBN 978-1-927409-63-3

~ GET YOUR COPY AT ~

ABLE MUSE PRESS: www.ablemusepress.com

OR

AMAZON WORLDWIDE: www.amazon.com

Able Muse – Print Edition, No. 19

SUMMER 2015

WITH

POETRY, FICTION, BOOK REVIEWS, INTERVIEWS & ESSAYS from wayne levin ▪ eric mchenry ▪ william baer ▪ catharine savage brosman ▪ susan mclean ▪ maura stanton ▪ meredith mccann ▪ len krisak ▪ bruce bennett ▪ linda boroff ▪ richard dokey ▪ robert earle ▪ kevin durkin ▪ eric torgersen ▪ cody walker ▪ and others

ISBN 978-1-927409-61-9

~ GET YOUR COPY AT ~

ABLE MUSE PRESS: www.ablemusepress.com

OR

AMAZON WORLDWIDE: www.amazon.com

*Able*MUSE
A REVIEW OF POETRY, PROSE & ART

After more than a decade of online publishing excellence, Able Muse began a bold new chapter with its Print Edition

Check out our 12+ years of online archives for work by

RACHEL HADAS ▪ X.J. KENNEDY ▪ TIMOTHY STEELE ▪ MARK JARMAN ▪ A.E. STALLINGS ▪ DICK DAVIS ▪ A.M. JUSTER ▪ TIMOTHY MURPHY ▪ ANNIE FINCH ▪ DEBORAH WARREN ▪ CHELSEA RATHBURN ▪ RHINA P. ESPAILLAT ▪ TURNER CASSITY ▪ RICHARD MOORE ▪ STEPHEN EDGAR ▪ DAVID MASON ▪ THAISA FRANK ▪ NINA SCHUYLER ▪ N.S. THOMPSON ▪ SOLITAIRE MILES ▪ MISHA GORDIN ▪ AND OTHERS

SUBSCRIPTION
Able Muse – Print Edition

Able Muse is published semiannually. *Subscription rates—for individuals:* $28.00 per year; single and previous issues: $19.95 + $3 S&H.

International subscription rates: $35 per year; single and previous issues: $19.95 + $5 S&H. (USD throughout.)

Subscribe online with WePay/credit card at

www.ablemusepress.com

Or send a check payable to *Able Muse Review*

Attn: Alex Pepple – Editor, *Able Muse*, 467 Saratoga Avenue #602, San Jose, CA 95129 USA

CONTENTS

FEATURED ARTIST

FICTION

POETRY

The Borrowed World

Poems

by Emily Leithauser

*NEW~ *from* Able Muse Press

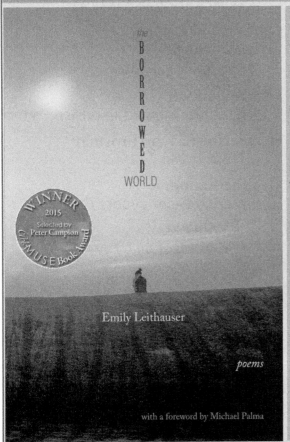

WINNER
2015 Able Muse Book Award

PRAISE FOR *THE BORROWED WORLD*
(with an foreword by Michael Palma)

First full-length collection from Emily Leithauser

★ ★ ★ ★ ★

The Borrowed World is [a] stunning debut.
— Natasha Thretewey, former US Poet Laureate

The Borrowed World marks the arrival of a major talent.
— Peter Campion
(Judge, 2015 Able Muse Book Award)

[Leithauser] transmutes perception into feeling, feeling into thought, and thought into revelation.
— Vijay Seshadri, winner of the Pulitzer Prize

[A] moving and memorable debut which covers a lot of ground but is always rooted in actualities.
— Andrew Motion, former UK Poet Laureate

Leithauser's art waits for you . . . you will be as pleased and moved by it as I have been.
— Michael Palma (from the foreword)

ISBN 978-1-927409-67-1 / 84 pages
ORDER NOW FROM ABLE MUSE PRESS AT: WWW.ABLEMUSEPRESS.COM
OR, ORDER FROM AMAZON.COM, BN.COM & OTHER ONLINE OR OFFLINE BOOKSTORES

www.AbleMusePress.com

Midge Goldberg

The Molt

I am not the creature but the shell.
I am not hiding but the space to hide,
the sturdy walls around a place to dwell.

At first my structure is a citadel—
the creature's safest when it stays inside.
I am not the creature but the shell,

yet as the creature grows, its needs compel
a sloughing off—my flaws are magnified.
My sturdy walls surround a place to dwell

but trapped inside this small a space is hell.
The creature leaves. The shell's unoccupied.
I am not the creature but the shell,

useless as when the clapper leaves the bell,
water the well. With nothing to provide,
my walls surround an empty place. I dwell

on whorling echoes, of nothing left to tell,
of no one left who ever laughed or cried.
I am not the creature but the shell,
the sturdy walls around a place to dwell.

Amit Majmudar

It's Time to Talk About Lord Byron Again

A Review of
Byron's Letters & Journals: A New Selection

Edited by Richard Lansdown, Oxford University Press, 2015
ISBN 978-0-19-872255-7, 518 pp., USA $50.00, hardcover

★ ★ ★

1.

IT'S TIME TO TALK ABOUT LORD BYRON again.

Apart from W.H. Auden, the twentieth century had little favorable to say about Byron. It was a century that privileged obscurity over wit and fragmentation over fluidity. Morally loose and/or politically radical poets were no longer "mad, bad, and dangerous to know"—in fact they became, and remain, rather commonplace.

Of course, the nineteenth century did plenty of talking about Byron, much of it while he was still alive. Enough talking, perhaps, and enough revering to make up for Byron's hundred-year spell as a second-tier Romantic, less knotty and footnotable than Coleridge, less youthful a corpse than Keats. Selling ten thousand copies of your poetry book is impressive by any standards. Doing it in 1814 London, whose population was no more than that of Dallas today—with a literacy rate a smidge over fifty percent—is even more impressive. To do all that *in a single day?* No wonder Sir Walter Scott (until Byron, Britain's bestselling poet) turned to historical fiction.

But Byron's fame was not merely breathless adulation from ladies of the aristocracy. His most extravagant praise came from extravagantly talented writers, many of them writers whose reputations aged far better than Byron's. In *Conversations with Eckermann,* we find Goethe in raptures over Byron's verse dramas; Keats and Wordsworth hardly registered with the Weimar sage. In a letter to a friend, the young Flaubert placed Byron in the same category as Shakespeare. Byron's reputation carried ever farther than across the Channel: Alexander Pushkin, the father of Russian poetry, had his start as an imitator of Byron in narratives such as "A Prisoner of the Caucasus."

The twentieth century was not so impressed. Although Byron figured in the aspirations of Joyce's Stephen Dedalus, T.S. Eliot accused Byron of possessing an "unphilosophical mind." Ironically enough, some of the best philosophers disagreed with that pronouncement. Nietzsche composed a whole "*Manfred* Meditation" for four hands at the piano. In *The Dawn,* he made no less than five references to Byron, twice mentioning the poet in the same breath as Napoleon. Nietzsche also felt the draw of Byron's informal prose; two of those five references come from Byron's diaries. Nietzsche quotes from *Manfred* in *Human, All Too Human,* a passage crucial enough for Bertrand Russell to transcribe it in his synopsis of the philosopher. ("The Tree of Knowledge," in case you're wondering, "is not the Tree of Life.") Whether Byron or any poet is truly "philosophical," we can set aside for now—what he is *not* is obscure or turgid, two qualities usually associated with "philosophical poetry," particularly of the Eliotic variety.

Tastes changed, as tastes do, and left Byron behind. In France, Baudelaire's *poète maudit* owed more than a little to the Byronic hero, but Symbolism emphasized the very characteristics Byron mocked in Coleridge's "Ancient Mariner." German taste, especially in the later twentieth century, turned to poets fundamentally un-Byronic, such as Celan.

Oddly, Soviet Russia alone kept alive that old Byronic veneration. *Don Juan* still enjoys canonical status in Russia, and the epic's most famous translation was made by one of Stalin's political prisoners, Tatiana Gnedich—entirely from memory. She was held in the cell alone, but with Byron's garrulous narrator for company, her confinement was far from solitary.

Don Juan was not Byron's only tragicomic epic. He wrote a second one, piecemeal, over the duration of his life, a true epic whose plot matches the plot of his own biography. Its hero lives a life more interesting than any Lake Poet's and dies a death more interesting than Shelley's. Byron wrote almost all of it down as it came to him. His Letters and Journals constitute, like *Don Juan,* this incomplete epic, one cut short by the author's death. A fresh and comprehensive selection, made by Richard Lansdown, is now published by Oxford University Press.

It's time to talk about Byron again.

2.

Ever since Byron's friend Thomas Moore published the first extracts from Byron's Letters in 1830, Byron's epistolary novel of a life has been best savored in a well-chosen selection. (The same holds true of his poetry; writers as prolific as Byron are never consistent.) The Byron biographer Leslie A. Marchand edited the complete letters for Harvard, but over thirteen volumes, even Byron's company flags. Marchand himself understood this and also prepared a selection. In fact, Byron's informal prose has invited scholar after scholar into a collaboration to filter and contextualize it. Lansdown is the most recent in a long line of Byron devotees.

The result is excellent and—this being the whole point of selection—very readable. Lansdown creates self-contained chapters by arranging most of the Letters geographically. Byron was a wanderer and exile for most of his later life, which fell neatly into phases: England, the Grand Tour, England again; then a series of Italian cities; and, finally, his fatal sojourn in Greece. Lansdown subdivides only where necessary, according to what Byron was writing. This helps him keep any one chapter from getting too long.

Each section is prefaced by a keen summary of the narrative background for the ensuing Letters. Lansdown picks out the best details, the catnip of gossip and coincidence—how Lady Caroline Lamb's cuckolded husband went on to be Victoria's first Prime Minister, how the last piece of fan mail Byron received came from none other than Johann Wolfgang von Goethe. (Byron's note of thanks was one of the few Letters that Lansdown should have included in its entirety. The irony of that letter was exquisite: Moments before embarking for Greece, Byron wrote that he considered Goethe's letter a "favourable omen" and promised to visit him in Weimar someday, "if I ever get back.")

Lansdown himself may be the Byronist to watch. He has written an entire book about the least-read part of Byron's oeuvre, the historical dramas, as well as work detailing Byron's involvement with a revolutionary movement in Ravenna, the Carbonari, in the 1820s. His afterword to this volume ends, "Leslie A. Marchand's . . . 1957 biography of the poet [is] still the best that has been published; perhaps it will not be improved upon." Based on that sentence, and knowing what I know of filial rivalries in scholarship and art alike, I suspect Mr. Lansdown is contemplating some mammoth biography of Byron that will out-Marchand Marchand. If so, consider my preorder placed.

3.

Are Byron's Letters as "good" as those of Keats? It depends on what we are looking for. Here we find no great insights into the poetic art and no sighing dreams of poetic fame. In fact, in the latter case, we get the opposite. Byron actually *possessed* poetic fame on a scale unimaginable beforehand, and he lived long enough to see that fame reverse its polarity and become infamy. As for insights into poetic art, Byron's Letters provide a corrective to Keats's: A poet does not have to have *any* particular insight into what he is doing. Byron, for example, did not know how to improve a poem if it did not come off right the first time: "I am like the tyger (in poesy) if I miss my first spring—I go growling back to my jungle."

Above all, though, Byron tramples on the hothouse-flower notion of "The Poet," whether one thinks of the tuberculous nightingale Keats, or Blake or Rilke eavesdropping on angels, or any latter-day botanizing academic. What Byron does is remind us it is possible for poetry to get written in the downtime between pleasure seeking and politicking, cussing and whoring and seeing (and saving) the world.

Byron's Letters have what you find in the letters of few other poets: *Tumult.* He sought drama, and drama sought him. A future Prime Minister's wife, jilted, cuts herself for his sake. A few months later, he's sleeping with his half-sister. White-water torrents in Switzerland, adultery in Italy; gonorrhea, malaria, indigestion. We read of him stripping off his coat and boots to keep Shelley, who was unable to swim, from drowning in a storm (he managed to pull the boat to shore in the end after vigorous bailing). Random gunshots sound a hundred feet from his door, after which he carries a dying policeman into his room to bleed to death. Enough action for one life, perhaps. Only then he sets off to expel the Turks from Greece . . . Byron may well be the Anti-Keats.

This may, in part, explain Byron's animus toward Keats and Wordsworth. I say "in part" because the other part seems to have been envy of elite-critical success; Byron's nastiest remarks about Keats were prompted by the sight of a glowing notice in the *Edinburgh Review,* which had savaged Byron's earliest book. "His [Keats's] is the very *Onanism* of poetry," wrote Byron, with the contempt of a man who never had to resort to it much. This sense of Keats as a writer primarily fixated on himself and his feelings, or rather making himself feel things, points up the contrast between the introvert and the extrovert. "O for a life of Sensations rather than of Thoughts!" wrote Keats in an 1817 letter to Benjamin Bailey. Byron later wrote to his publisher John Murray, defending the profoundly un-Keatsian *Don Juan:* "Is it not life? Is it not the *thing?*" And earlier in 1813 Byron had written to Annabella Milbanke, his future wife, that "The great object of life is Sensation—to feel that we exist—even though in pain—it is this 'craving void' which drives us to Gaming—to Battle—to Travel—to intemperate but keenly felt pursuits of every description."

Although the two poets agreed about "sensation," it was in two totally different ways— one focused inward, the other focused outward; one writing the Odes, the other a garrulous satirist. One became the poet of sensation. The other became a sensation himself.

In Keats, the letters seem to precede the poetic development, exhibiting a depth of thought and at times a power of expression in advance of the poetry. Much of our sense of what was lost with Keats's death is actually the mind we glimpse in the letters, that paradoxically *metaphysical sensuality* whose poetic expressions are those famous Odes. With Byron, this relationship between the letters and the poetry holds, too, and because Byron's destiny was toward *conversational music* (what else is *Don Juan?*), that is what we get in the Letters.

Consider this phrase tossed off to his half-sister, in which he gives us some double alliteration and slips into iambic meter:

> . . . independent as a German Prince who coins his own Cash, or a Cherokee Chief who coins no Cash at all . . .

It is crucial to recall that this letter was written in 1808, almost coevally with his desultory juvenilia, *Hours of Idleness.* This musical spontaneity will be inaccessible to Byron the versifier for some years yet; a prodigious amount of deliberate, stylized verse will intervene. Only a decade later, in the ottava rima of *Don Juan,* will the poet Byron catch up and superimpose on the Byron of the Letters. It is in *Don Juan,* the unfinished poem at the end of Byron's poetic career, that the qualities on glorious display in the Letters are found from the very start: the dashed-off felicity of phrase, wild tonal variation, irreverence, an omnium-gatherum approach to subject matter and the personal voice. These occur naturally in the Letters, but Byron had to overcome great obstacles to attain them in his poetry.

4.

WHAT WERE THOSE OBSTACLES? His audience, for one. Contemporary readers in England wanted more Oriental Romances, not the worldly garrulity of *Don Juan.* From the very beginning, early nineteenth-century assumptions about what a good poem looked like guided (and misguided) Byron's poetic output. The descriptions of his tour of Albania and Turkey in the Letters show his close observation and knack for matching form to content. Consider the crowd of clauses with which he describes the crowded court of Ali Pasha in Tepelana:

> The Albanians in their dresses (the most magnificent in the world, consisting of a long white kilt, gold worked cloak, crimson velvet gold laced jacket and waistcoat, silver mounted pistols and daggers), the Tartars with their high caps, the Turks in their vast pelisses and turbans, the soldiers and black slaves with the horses, the former stretched in groups in an immense open gallery in front of the palace, the latter placed in a kind of cloister below it, two hundred steeds ready caparisoned to move in a moment, couriers entering or passing out with dispatches, the kettle drums beating, boys calling the hour from the minaret of the mosque . . .

Byron uses this raw material when he sets about writing *Childe Harold*, but instead of being heightened or focused, the scene is rendered diffuse and generic:

> Richly caparisoned, a ready row
> Of armed horse, and many a warlike store,
> Circled the wide-extending court below;
> Above, strange groups adorned the corridor;
> And ofttimes through the area's echoing door,
> Some high-capped Tartar spurred his steed away;
> The Turk, the Greek, the Albanian, and the Moor,
> Here mingled in their many-hued array,
> While the deep war-drum's sound announced the close of day.
>
> The wild Albanian kirtled to his knee,
> With shawl-girt head and ornamented gun,
> And gold-embroidered garments, fair to see:
> The crimson-scarfed men of Macedon;
> The Delhi with his cap of terror on,
> And crooked glaive; the lively, supple Greek;
> And swarthy Nubia's mutilated son;
> The bearded Turk, that rarely deigns to speak,
> Master of all around, too potent to be meek,
>
> Are mixed conspicuous: some recline in groups,
> Scanning the motley scene that varies round;
> There some grave Moslem to devotion stoops,
> And some that smoke, and some that play are found;
> Here the Albanian proudly treads the ground;
> Half-whispering there the Greek is heard to prate;
> Hark! from the mosque the nightly solemn sound,
> The muezzin's call doth shake the minaret,
> "There is no god but God!—to prayer—lo! God is great!"

This is early Byron, making all the wrong decisions: syntactical inversions, archaisms, substituting a war-drum for a kettle-drum, making the object *harder* to visualize; and making sure a muezzin is minaret-shakingly (!) calling Muslims to prayer (which is what English readers expected in a poem about the Islamic world), instead of just "boys calling the hour."

By *Don Juan*, the formality would be gone—and the form would be perfected. The familiar and cheeky tone of his letters to college cronies like John Cam Hobhouse would be cast in an ottava rima that swaggered on light feet. Byron's memory of Turkish dress would find a place there, but in *Don Juan* such memories would be focused and quickened:

A Candiote cloak, which to the knee might reach,
    And trousers not so tight that they would burst,
But such as fit an Asiatic breech;
    A shawl, whose folds in Cashmire had been nurst,
Slippers of saffron, dagger rich and handy;
In short, all things which form a Turkish Dandy.

5.

OF COURSE, BY THE TIME BYRON STRUCK OUT on his various exiles, he was every inch the aristocrat, a class of people who did not fetch their own coats from the closet. Whether exiled, disgraced, or battling the Turks in the name of Hellas, certain things simply did not change. So Byron, even when thousands of pounds in debt, traveled with his share of servants, and wrote home complaining how their coarseness interfered with his raptures over the Alpine scenery.

He much preferred his animals. Byron had kept a bear on a leash while in college, but by the time of his Italian sojourn, the entourage had grown to include—among other creatures—a badger, a crow, a monkey, an Egyptian crane, and a fox, not to mention the usual cats and dogs. What with the prolific poetizing, the bisexual vortex of his bed set amid the smells and noises of a small zoo, the international fame, the international infamy, the looks, and the wealth, he must have struck people as a monster of nature, possessing a kind of preternaturally intense life-force.

It is hard to put a number on Byron's women, to tally the wives of all classes, serving-girls, and whores who shared his bed. If we are to believe his reports—in one letter he mentions over a hundred liaisons in a single year—a decade in Italy would have seen him surpassing Don Giovanni's *mille e tre*. The promiscuity at times did wax operatic, if only opéra bouffe, complete with shouting matches between the weeping cuckold and the defiant adulteress, whilst the foreign interloper buttoned his breeches. In 1817, one of Byron's mistresses moved into his house uninvited and refused to leave, even after her husband, her relatives, the police, and Byron himself begged her to go home. (He ended up employing her as a housekeeper-with-benefits; apparently she performed excellently in both her duties, reducing his daily expenses by half.) To gauge how sordid Byron got in those years, we need only go to the Letters of his neighbor and fellow exile, Percy Bysshe Shelley—who, for all his atheism and his shared contempt for British moral cant, was horrified to hear Byron haggle with Italian parents over the price of their daughter.

The safest sex Byron had was with other men's wives, except for the wildly unstable Lady Caroline Lamb. Speaking of psychiatric pathology, as Byron's liaisons pile up his promiscuity comes to seem somewhat diseased or sick and not just with the clap (which, admittedly, he did contract). Byron's behavior exceeds that of the usual "handsome rake" at play among the notoriously louche British aristocracy. Byron had numerous partners of both sexes and all social classes in several countries.

Reading the Letters, it comes across as rather *hectic*. From the perspective of modern psychiatry, Byron showed the self-endangering hypersexuality often exhibited by victims of childhood sexual abuse. ("Self-endangering," literally, since homosexuality was a hanging offense in nineteenth-century Britain. Incest, by contrast, got you six months.) It comes as no surprise to learn that Byron was "sexually interfered with" (Lansdown's phrase) by his nurse, May Gray, over the course of several months. He was nine years old when it started. This underemphasized trauma may be why Byron, years later, *inverted the Don Juan myth*. His Juan remains an innocent youth, not the seducer but the one seduced; women, frequently older and more experienced ones, are the predators.

6.

THAT PRETERNATURAL LIFE-FORCE WAS ALWAYS THREATENING to turn into its opposite. Over-the-top Byronic promiscuity is never far from the blackest depression. (In our day, for example, porn stars attempt or commit suicide more often than the general population.) In Byron, though, the suicide-impulse was matched by an equally powerful joie de vivre. The two reconciled and hybridized into the wish to be *reborn*.

More than once—beginning in 1810 with his *Childe Harold* tourism, actually—he sought a way to erase his past and start over in some new, nobler, purer way. His flight to Italy was another attempt to escape his past, or as he tellingly referred to it, his "*life in England*" (emphasis mine, deathwish his). Within a year of his ongoing Italian orgy, he started contemplating ways of annihilating himself. Lansdown gives us a long letter in which Byron tries to make the legal and economic arrangements to settle in Bolivar's South America. The increasingly pudgy aristocrat was many things, but a spade and plow man he was not, and we hear no more about the scheme. Nevertheless, this new identity is not so easily dismissed as fantasy, given what we know about his eventual "rebirth" as a commander of Greek rebel forces. He really *was* that eager for a new life—that is, for death. Escaping to occupied Greece was one more way for Byron to kill off Byron while still enjoying boys and hock.

And yet. Byron's self-transformation—his self-overcoming, in Nietzschean terms—seems genuine, judging from the last section of Letters. The jaded, rapidly aging nobleman broke through to actual nobility. These last Letters constitute at once the least salacious and most fascinating group. Gone are the petty sniping, the boastful vulgarity, the self-pity. (His literary productivity, alas, went with them.) In their place, we get instructions to bankers arranging loans for the cause, clear-eyed assessments of Greek mendacity, and accounts of close escapes from capture by the Turkish fleet.

Byron's problems in Missolonghi seem bitterly familiar: mercenary tribes, more interested in foreign money than national independence; endless internal squabbles among half a dozen would-be George Washingtons; questions of equipment and training and trust. Americans would encounter the same intractable factors when trying to "nation-build" in the fractured, fractious areas of Afghanistan and Iraq—only they had the advantage of being the empire. Byron paid for his weapons and soldiers out of his own pocket.

7.

SHELLEY, WHOM YEATS WOULD LATER COMPARE to an angel, lay decomposing for ten days in the Gulf of Spezia before his body was washed up. The author of *Adonais* could be identified only by the volume of Keats in his pocket. (An initial report claimed it was a Bible, perhaps to suggest the wild-eyed atheist had been coming around to Christian belief before the end.) The body was cremated on the beach, and Byron reports, with all the deadpan delivery of Gabriel García Márquez, the magical-realist fact of how Shelley's heart did not burn, "and is now preserved in spirits of wine."

Shelley took four hours to burn down completely. Byron, as if to undrown his friend, went for a three-mile swim in the sea while the pyre smoked on the shore. Shirtless in the afternoon sun, Byron, too, burned. When he emerged—"scorched and drenched," as Lansdown points out—he began the slow process of blistering. For days, he could not lay on his back or flank, and eventually the skin sloughed. Byron described himself as "St. Bartholomewed," referring to the patron saint of the Armenian Church, martyred by being flayed alive. (Among Byron's more interesting side projects was a collaboration with Armenian monks to produce a grammar of their language.) That image of death was followed, shortly afterward, by an image of rebirth: "But now I have a new skin, though it is * * * * tender." Byron, the most graphomaniacal of the Romantics, shortly after this self-baptism-cum-sympathetic-cremation, stopped producing.

He did return to writing for the occasional poem, like the much-anthologized one about reaching his thirty-sixth year. Still, the last year of his life, like Shakespeare's, was mostly one of willed silence, or of the failure to will verse. "Composition," he wrote in 1823, "is a habit of my mind," but it proved the first habit he broke to effect his metamorphosis, or his rebirth.

8.

BY THIS TIME, OF COURSE, he had already produced a body of work that, unlike Wordworth's or Keats's, remains too various and vast to describe as a whole. Byron the man can be analyzed and generalized about; Byron the writer, the *whole* writer, defies any critic.

Byron was easily the most ambitious of all the European Romantics—perhaps the most ambitious writer of the nineteenth century, barring Victor Hugo and Goethe, both of whose literary ambition included non-poetic forms (and both of whose lives and Letters are not nearly as interesting).

Zoom out and observe how, *within a mere ten years,* Byron stormed almost every imaginable type and genre of poetry: the lyric, the narrative, and the dramatic; within narrative and lyric poetry, both Romance and satire, and within drama, both the history play (like *The Two Foscari)* and the religious/Biblical mystery.

Dates of composition suggest *Cain* was composed during a lull between Cantos of *Don Juan.* This toggling between the worldly-coarse and the mythopoetic would not be seen again until James Joyce, who knew better than to go fully mythic and bring his otherworldly beings onstage, as it were. Joyce kept his mythic material covered with, coded into, his Dublin and his Dubliners. Byron, by contrast, wanted to be everything in full, with no concessions to the expectations of the age.

Because he had *done* the spirit of the age. In his last years, he wanted to become utterly untimely (*unzeitgemäße,* as Nietzsche used to say). Byron wanted to be a neoclassical satirist like Pope *and* the Miltonic bard of the Beyond. Granted, Byron succeeded at his satirical project and failed to nail his Miltonic one—but Milton's Biblical blank verse sublime has escaped everyone, even Milton himself in *Paradise Regain'd.*

This breadth is what makes generalizing about Byron's oeuvre so difficult. What can be said of his satires, positive or negative, cannot be said of the blank verse plays; what can be said of the blank verse plays cannot be said of the Oriental Romances. The haunted "Byronic hero" of *Manfred* is nowhere to be found in *Don Juan.* The Letters alone, showing us Byron's rapid-fire multiplicity, possess a breadth and variety equal to the *Complete Poems.* In fact, his worst poetry seems to be the stuff that has no parallel or context in his life and Letters. You can't imagine this letter-writer also writing *Sardanapalus.*

9.

YOU CAN, HOWEVER, IMAGINE THE BYRON of the Letters writing *Don Juan.* So readily, in fact, it is hard to understand why his closest associates were so turned off by it.

As for the readership at large, it is rather more understandable. Byron's reputation followed a few typical patterns of fame. Sudden adulation suddenly reversed its polarity. One month he was the embodiment of Poesy complete with a dimple in the chin; the next he was an incestuous devil, complete with a limp. His contemporaries were utterly incapable of balanced appraisals when it came to him.

The other typical pattern relates to his literary fame, or rather why it cooled: He stayed a bestseller even in disgrace and exile, so long as he kept churning out Oriental Romances, but when he broke with the pattern, no one wanted this new *risus sardonicus* Byron. Shelley was the one of the few who saw the poem for the masterpiece it was; in fact, the boat that capsized in the Gulf of Spezia was named the *Don Juan*. Most poets claim indifference to public reaction, then anguish over a nasty review. Byron claimed indifference, too, but as it turns out, he actually *meant* it. The Letters show us how, just as Byron hit on his true theme and style as a poet, people around him started turning on his masterpiece—even John Murray, who had made a killing off of Byron's earlier works; even Countess Theresa Guiccioli, who was sleeping with him. This happened *while Byron was still writing it*. Each set of two or three Cantos met with leery distaste and recommendations for cuts before it even saw print.

Judging from his own testimony, Byron would have left off *Don Juan* if so many friends and strangers had not booed it. He knocked out sixteen Cantos and the opening part of a seventeenth, admirably self-assured about its worth, channeling perhaps that new kid who had arrived in London years earlier with a Scottish accent and a limp.

> I care nothing for what may be the consequence—critical or otherwise—all the bullies on earth shall not prevent me from writing what I like—& publishing what I like—"coute qui coute" [cost what it may]—if they had let me alone—I probably should not have continued beyond the five first—as it is—there shall be such a poem—as has not been since Ariosto—in length—in satire—in imagery—and in what I please.—

Why have the Letters, and *Don Juan*, aged so much better than vast tracts of Byron's other poetic work? Like Coleridge, but unlike the other English Romantics, Byron created dramatic scenes and situations that were *separable from their language*. Compare Keats's urn, or Wordsworth's daffodils: there, the beauty of the language is the truth of the poetry, and the two cannot be separated. In much of Byron's High Romantic work, imaginative force compensated for a lack of linguistic force. *The Corsair* was written in one hot week, and a reader today can tell. The style and power are in the teller and the tale—not in the telling.

Don Juan, by contrast, has aged so well precisely because of the narrator's leisurely disinterest in his own story. He is far more interested in his rhymes, digressions, and epigrammatic clinchers—in other words, the *words*. Byron's great comic epic was produced just as quickly as his other works, but what makes those other works seem half-thought-out makes *Don Juan* seem effervescent. Haste and inattention free up his tongue to do what it does best.

The same principle is at play in the Letters, with their incorporation of foreign phrases, associative leaps divided by proto-Dickinsonian dashes, and lucid ludic prowess. In the Letters, too, we find abrupt riffs and dilations where extemporaneous linguistic delight takes over. Associations tumble out of him. When a review expresses distaste for *Don Juan*'s mode-mixing—"We are never scorched and drenched whilst standing in the same spot"—Byron seizes on the metaphor to accumulate an energetic, profane, chockablock little catalogue.

> Blessings on his experience! Ask him these questions about "scorching and drenching." Did he never play at cricket, or walk a mile in hot weather? Did he never spill a dish of tea over himself in handing the cup to his charmer, to the great shame of his nankeen breeches? Did he never swim in the sea at noonday with the sun in his eyes and on his head, which all the foam of ocean could not cool? Did he never draw his foot out of too hot water, damning his eyes and his valet's? Did he never tumble into a river or lake, fishing, and sit in his wet clothes in the boat, or on the bank, afterwards "scorched and drenched," like a true sportsman?

Shakespeare, too, suffered the disapproval of later critics for mixing comedy and tragedy. Byron's Letters from day to day, like Shakespeare's dramas from scene to scene, vary genres and moods. Byron the letter-writer was not above skipping up into rhymes, just as Shakespeare did not hesitate to dash off a scene in prose. Both writers approximate the alternations of life as it is lived.

That riff I quoted, triggered by a trivial critique, is not the sort of thought, tone, or blithe vulgarity that could be cast in a conventional nineteenth-century English poem. Or a poem in *any* tradition, really, save the comic/bawdy tradition (which is not quite the same as "light verse"). This tradition, often linked to satire, can be found in parts of Chaucer, in those bits of Shakespeare most often cut by directors, and in the bawdy doggerel of many an otherwise prim poet's private letters, including T.S. Eliot's. In *Don Juan*, a comic, bawdy, inspired vulgarity surfaced shamelessly. It dove to wait out the Victorians, and then made a verbal spectacle of itself again in Joyce's *Ulysses*.

Byron had something in his nature that was alien to the Ode or the blank verse meditation or sighing romance—yet it was not something "unpoetic," or rather, only the poetic culture deemed it so (and still does). While he expressed it immortally in *Don Juan*, he expressed it first in the Letters.

10.

THE RISK OF READING A POET'S BIOGRAPHY OR LETTERS is that you may discover things about the poet that make you hate him. As Victorian England became even more prudish and pious, Byron fell into disrepute as a womanizer and a godless type. He had heroized Cain and given English literature its first and, to my knowledge, only sympathetic treatment of incest—Manfred is tormented, yes, but you're still meant to feel for him. The Letters don't contradict these impressions. Once, severely ill on his first visit to Greece, he scared off the priests and their extreme unction by threatening to "turn Mussalman if they come again." And his half-sister Augusta seems to be one of the few women he truly loved, both as a brother and as something more.

Byron's anticlericalism is rather commonplace among contemporary intellectuals, and his doomed relationship with his half-sister seems more tragic than shocking. And so we can see through to a different Byron in these Letters. Take his relationship with Coleridge, for example. In a letter soliciting Byron's help, Coleridge compared Byron to a swan and himself to a cygnet taken under Byron's wing. He wanted Byron to lean on his publisher, John Murray, to give him a publishing contract. Byron's reply was full of generous praise, and sure enough, Murray ended up publishing *Christabel and Other Poems* the next year. Coleridge's next volume was no great score for the publisher of Scott and Austen, but Murray could afford to do Byron this favor: Murray paid Byron well for rights to his poems, but his star author, even when in debt (and he was always in debt), steadfastly refused to accept royalty checks for his bestsellers.

Byron did not stop there. Within a few days, he was urging his friend Thomas Moore, the once-bestselling, now-forgotten Irish poet, to review Coleridge favorably on the book's release: "I do think he [Coleridge] only wants a Pioneer and a sparkle or two to explode most gloriously." While Byron the satirist made the occasional quip at the *Ancient Mariner*'s expense—"I wish he would explain his explanation"—Byron the man proved supportive and generous, and Coleridge remained grateful. Decades later, Coleridge's grandson went on to coedit Byron's thirteen-volume *Complete Works*.

Coleridge was not the only poet he helped. After the *Don Juan* capsized in the Gulf of Spezia, Byron wrote, aristocrat to aristocrat, to Shelley's estranged father, securing an allowance for the poet's widow.

Byron also seems free of the prejudices, like anti-Semitism, typical of his time and class. His Scottish ancestry, his clubfoot, and his bisexuality seem to have immunized him against such things. In 1814, at the height of his fame, Byron collaborated with two Jewish musicians, eventually publishing the volume *Hebrew Melodies*. "The Destruction of Sennacherib," a common classroom text, emerged from this collaboration. A few days before Byron—in disgrace, messily separated from his wife, barred from seeing his baby daughter—was driven out of Britain, the composer Isaac Nathan sent him, as a gift for his journey, a package of matzos.

Byron wanted to be buried in Greece, but his companions brought his body back to England. In one of those symbolic details that would look terribly heavy-handed in a novel, the sexual sinner was buried at the church of St. Mary Magdalene.

He had been famous during his lifetime, but fame does not quite describe what happened to him after his death. Byron went from Britain's most famous poet to a pan-European phenomenon. He crossed over from literary history into the history of *history books,* as the countless comparisons between him and Napoleon reveal. How did this come about?

His backstory and his looks did not have as much to do with it as one would think. Paradoxically, it was the writing—even some of the worst writing. Notice that many of his most enthusiastic admirers among other writers were writers from other languages. Only Shakespeare traveled better. Both poets crossed languages and cultures so well because their effects were not limited to nuances of language alone—that is, their poetry derived its effect from elements that *were not* lost in translation. The histrionics of Hamlet leaping into Ophelia's grave, or Othello stabbing Desdemona, have their counterparts in the Byronic hero springing a princess from a Turkish harem, or Manfred brooding on a mountaintop. Such scenes and situations, products of Byron's highly dramatic imagination, could be shelled from their original language and still captivate.

So a year after Giuseppe Verdi made a grand opera out of *Macbeth,* he made one out of Byron's *The Corsair (Il corsaro, 1848).* So did Berlioz, incidentally; Adolphe Adam, better known as the composer of *Giselle,* made a ballet of it. All three *Corsair*-based productions premiered between 1844 and 1856, defying the usual pattern in which a famous writer's reputation declines after his death. 1844 also witnessed the publication of the bestseller by Alexandre Dumas in which Edmund Dantès returns as the Count of Monte Cristo—a rich and haunted nobleman who loves dressing in Turkish clothes and is repeatedly compared to Byron, both by the author himself and by fascinated characters in the book.

As the century progressed, Byron's lineage hurled forth larger-than-life figures whose lives and careers, consciously or unconsciously, paralleled or reflected elements of Byron's. The Byron who fought alongside natives in native dress, for freedom from the Ottoman Empire, had a human echo one hundred years later in T.E. Lawrence. Lawrence even shared Byron's philhellenism, translating the *Odyssey* while on campaign.

Lawrence's great difference with Byron was his sexually repressed lifestyle; some of his contemporaries believed him to be asexual. The European seducer in dashing exotic garb, however, rode again as Rudy Valentino as *The Son of the Sheikh.* One Western cultural infatuation echoed the other. Simply compare photographs of Valentino as an Arab with Thomas Phillips's portrait of Byron in Albanian costume, which happens to be on the cover of Lansdown's selection. You will see how Byron settled into the collective memory of the West.

The Byron whose unapologetic sexual deviance flaunted British mores and British law, resulting in disgrace and exile, lived and loved again in Oscar Wilde. Both men, neither one an Englishman, died in exile from the London that had toasted their brilliance. Wilde's talent, like Byron's, flourished when he pursued art forms that showcased wit and epigrammatic flair. Like Byron, Wilde utterly underperformed the moment he attempted a Poetic Drama on a Religious Theme (in Wilde's case, *Salomé*).

Among contemporary poets, it is hard to find a single poet whose life or work has anything Byronic about it. Partly this has to do with how poetry, generally, has turned inward and rather solemn. We are, in this respect, the descendants of Wordsworth and Keats. The unifying characteristic of Byron's poetry in any of his genres—lyric, narrative romance, satire—is that it's freewheeling. This is why, at its worst, it is slapdash, while at its best, it has spontaneity, serendipity, *sprezzatura*.

We have had no Byronic poet for a few generations now, and we are the duller for it. Luckily for us, this situation is not without remedy. It is time to talk about Lord Byron again. It is also time to read him again, and I recommend Lansdown's *Selected Letters and Journals* as an excellent place to start.

Jean L. Kreiling

"Waiting for the Return of the Fishing Fleet"

After Winslow Homer

She knows the truth—that she may wait
with us for hours, that he'll be late,
that this raw light will burn her eyes,
that she'll grow weary as she tries
for patience, that sometimes she'll hate

the sea that he must navigate,
the sun that will illuminate
its bitter sparkle and its size—
she knows. The truth

is that if she should choose a mate
like ours, she'll learn the awful weight
of water, as love amplifies
the depths of fear. Though now she cries,
"There's Daddy!" and we celebrate,
she knows the truth.

Jean L. Kreiling

Six Inventions after J.S. Bach

Contrapuntal Bliss

Two-Part Invention No. 1, BWV 772

One starts, the other follows, they are never
apart for long, and nobody can sever
the tangled paths on which they romp and run;
their contrapuntal bond can't be undone.
Although the solemn vows were never said,
what Bach has joined together will stay wed.

Pitched Battle

Two-Part Invention No. 6, BWV 777

The conflict cannot be resolved: each rise
is countered by descent. Though each line tries
to see the other's point—they switch positions—
the argument persists, and repetitions
make clear that no one wins, no one submits,
and no one minds this clash of opposites.

Vacillation

Two-Part Invention No. 12, BWV 783

Stay where you are—trill prettily, but stay—
or wander wantonly, carouse and play.
Or can you be both resolute and brisk,
be faithful as you dare to take a risk?
Why not? Learn how to sprint, how to be still,
how much might tremble in a pretty trill.

18

Competition

Three-Part Invention No. 4, BWV 790

"Here's how it's done: dip down, leap up, repeat."
"Oh, I can beat that, and not miss a beat."
"No, listen, friends, here's how it ought to go;
I make it more seductive—lush and low."
Three voices vie, each phrase gently debated,
the whole impeccably coordinated.

Late Autumn

Three-Part Invention No. 7, BWV 793

Late autumn weeps—its rhythms nearly spent,
its pitches tracing arcs of discontent,
its woven colors muted but united
in intricate devotions unrequited.
Life, death, and splendor sigh in synchrony:
the season's bittersweet polyphony.

Love Triangle

Three-Part Invention No. 15, BWV 801

Perhaps three parts are really one too many:
of all these close-knit measures, hardly any
allow the voices to sing equally—
there's always one who waits his turn to be
a part of this romance. While two hearts race,
a third marks time, left out of the embrace.

Sankha Ghosh

Which Side Are You On?

"Tumi Kon Dale?"

Before you extend a hand to the man
running after the speeding bus,
ask him which party he belongs to.
Before you raise a morsel to any
hunger-stricken mouth, ask
about the man's party affiliation.
Before you pick up the body that
police-fire has dropped on the pavement,
check his true allegiance.
Your own hands may be besmirched
in blood, but nevertheless, do
check the colors on everyone else's;
and when inside a dark tunnel, don't
forget to light the torch that helps
spot foreheads marked by telltale tattoos.
Deeds and what people are actually
saying must not take precedence over
the cards they carry (or fail to).
Stray cases of deaths, beheadings
in remote villages really should not
bother you so much; instead, take in
our solidarity, join our wild, frenzied
dance party—dum dee da da dum—
exploring the lower depths tonight.
Before the highest court passes
any verdict, sworn statements must

be taken on the defendant's leanings.
Even the carcass must be unhung from
its self-squeezing noose and the query
must be whispered in its ears.
And, before you turn in, before
you make love, do remember to ask:
"Which side, dear, which side are *you* on?"

— *Translated from the Bengali[1] of Sankha Ghosh
by Ani Dasgupta*

---

1   See "Translation Notes" on page 133 for the original Bengali poem.

Ron McFarland

Digressions

I WAS READING SOME SORT OF FUTURISTIC FANTASY, or allegory, or maybe it was a parable about a New Israel and a New Jerusalem replete with simulacra and set on some distant planet, when I found my mind rambling backwards into the past, nearly fifty years ago, and the fact that it was quite content to find itself back in Urbana, Illinois, in July or August 1968, probably explains as well as anything does why it is that I've never been a fan of sci-fi or premise fiction. It's outrageous, when you think of it, for a "serious reader" to allow himself that sort of self-indulgent segue, at the very least an insult to the writer who, in the present case, was quite good. And yet, I seem to be embarking on these unwarranted but oddly satisfying mental rambles more and more frequently of late. Maybe it's the weather.

Malcolm was a fellow graduate student plugging away on his doctorate in that hot, humid Midwest summer. I forget his dissertation topic. Mine would concern a minor seventeenth-century British poet, but I didn't know that at the time. All I knew was that my subject would be something from that era and my directing professor would probably be Arthur E. Barker, whose book *Milton and the Puritan Dilemma* I had bought in what then seemed a hugely expensive hardbound edition. Professor Barker was on sabbatical at the time, and I had never met him, but I glibly and naively assumed he would take me under his wing, which he did. Malcolm was working on something in American lit, I think, maybe with Nina Baym, who was then one of the new kids on the block at UI. The University of Illinois at Champaign-Urbana was into what we called the Star System back then, maybe still is, maybe all of the really good universities are, and Nina Baym was going to be a star, like Arthur Barker.

Of course most of that paragraph was a digression.

Malcolm, whose actual name was not Malcolm but Malachi, pronounced with emphasis on the second syllable, was from

22

Israel, but his family was British and had been there when it was Palestine, before the partition in 1947 and the outbreak of war in 1948. His name means "God's messenger," and the Book of Malachi just barely makes it into the Christian Old Testament. I'm no biblical scholar, or even a churchgoer, and I wasn't back then either, but I read the four quick chapters just out of curiosity after Malcolm told me about his name. It wasn't exactly a breakthrough text for me. Malachi (which I'd always pronounced with stress on the first syllable and the terminal "i" rhyming with "high" instead of "see") scolds the Israelites, but that's no revelation—that's what Old-Testament prophets do—and there are textual hints at the coming messiah, but those aren't revelatory either. The six verses that comprise the fourth chapter are the best from where I sit: "For behold, the day cometh, that shall burn as an oven; and all the proud, yea, and all that do wickedly, shall be stubble: and the day that cometh shall burn them up, saith the Lord of hosts, that it shall leave them neither root nor branch."

Back then I was doing all of my bible reading in the King James Version because it debuted in 1611 and was the obviously pertinent translation for a student of mid-seventeenth-century British lit. Even today, unrepentant nonchurchgoer that I continue to be, I find the KJV seductive. Something about the wicked being reduced to "stubble" appeals to me. Out here in Idaho, which is where I ended up after my Illini days, the farmers burn off the wheat stubble every fall, allergy sufferers and asthmatics be damned. And it appeals to my perverse nature to

think of the Old Testament as ending with a threat from the Almighty: "Lest I come and smite the earth with a curse." Well, of course—and how appropriate, too, that the very last word of the Old Testament would be "curse."

Right off, I should say that it could not concern me less if some biblical scholar might insist that the KJV translators had it all wrong, that the last word of the Old Testament should be "blessing," or that the last phrase should be "the heart of the children to their fathers." And anyway, this was just another digression.

What I recalled as I was reading that futuristic fiction (be it fantasy, allegory, parable, or somehow all of the above) was that intensely muggy evening when Malcolm invited a few of us over to his third-floor apartment to see some slides he'd brought back from his visit home, to the Promised Land, in June, just one year after the astonishing Six-Day War that had pitted lone Israel, not twenty years old as a nation, against the combined might of Egypt, Syria, and Jordan, along with the support of Arabs and Muslims everywhere, from Algeria to Sudan and including Pakistan. Malcolm had been in England at the time, maybe at Oxford. I forget. Most Americans and Westerners, Europeans and otherwise, regarded the war as a classic David versus Goliath affair, and I confess to having been as naive as any when it came to what was going on in that part of the world despite the advantage of having taken a fascinating course in Near East history when I was an undergraduate. By any standards the result was remarkable. Outnumbered in tanks and aircraft by at least three to one and by ground troops more than two to one, the Israelis not only repelled the invaders, but in fierce fighting they managed to sweep the Sinai Peninsula right up to the Suez Canal and to seize the Gaza Strip, the strategic Golan Heights overlooking Syria, and Jordan's West Bank. General Moshe Dayan emerged as the great hero of the moment with Egypt's Gamal Abdel Nasser as the arch-villain. Arriving in Urbana in the fall of 1967 after two years of teaching in Texas and having grown up in a fairly small town in Florida, I was struck by the large number of proud Jewish students. Every pretty Jewish coed I saw seemed to be celebrating the stunning June victory with her Star of David blue eyeshadow and bright white eyeliner. I suppose it was just the style at the time, but I saw something political and patriotic about it. Of course I knew even less about Judaism than I did about the realities of life in Israel and the Middle East, but I had dated a couple of Jewish girls somewhere along the line (Jane and Ellen, to be specific), and of course had fallen in love with both of them. Back then I pretty much fell in love with any girl, or woman, who would go out with me more than twice.

In the spring of 1968 I signed up for a course in Modern Hebrew, which was being offered at UI for the first time, as I understood it. I even went so far as to inquire into (as opposed to "study" or bring myself to "understand") the alphabet. Why I did this, I have no idea. I've always been interested in languages, though, and by that time I'd taken at least a smattering of Latin,

Spanish, Russian, German, and French, even a dab of Attic Greek. Hebrew seemed like a good idea. But as it happened, the course was oversubscribed, and knowing that my interest was in the nature of mere infatuation, I bowed out so that more earnest students could have my place. Hasn't this also been a digression of sorts?

Back to the sweltering evening at Malcolm's apartment with my wife and a dozen other grad students, mostly from the English department. Lined up on the kitchen counter were a few dozen bottles of beer, carefully hauled out of the icy cold of his refrigerator so they might be consumed British fashion at room temperature. I'd heard of that practice, but had never before witnessed it, let alone suffered from it. The practice still seems wrong to me, an insult to good lager. And then came the slides. The tiny apartment was not air-conditioned. The small windows were open as wide as they'd go, and as I recall, there was a halfhearted fan of some sort.

As I remember them the slides were dazzling, but too numerous. They would not stop. It was if they had some mystical, mesmeric grip on Malcolm. Could there have been hundreds? It seemed like thousands at the time, and they were dazzling in several ways: the tremendous variety, the startling desert landscape with its sharp, bright aridity, the great blue Mediterranean as seen from Haifa, the images of burned out and abandoned tanks and armored cars, orthodox Jews praying at the Wailing Wall, dancing kibbutzniks, Tel Aviv by moonlight, what seemed mere boys and girls from the kibbutzim armed and on guard or drilling, the golden Dome of the Rock, coffee shops that could have been those I'd seen in Miami, and then acres and acres of grapes, or hay, or cotton, or oranges, olive groves, date palms. We were all pretty much crammed into that tight room, and my wife and I were unfortunately seated, so we could not escape the projector's bright glare. The stark Israeli sun bore down on us slide after slide.

Somewhere along the line Malcolm put on some Israeli music, but predictably the only piece I can recall is the familiar "Hava Nagila," which translates as "Let Us Rejoice." My wife was not rejoicing but was acquiring a splitting headache, and although I never suffer from headaches, I'm pretty sure I was heading in that direction when she insisted we leave. We were the first to go, and I could tell Malcolm was offended, but it was too late for me to take it back—I'd already said we had to go, mumbled something about a babysitter. We didn't even have a baby. That would be the next year, 1969. Malcolm's pretty young wife, whose English was not very good, seemed hurt. Later, I heard, there was dancing and a strong liqueur called arak that tastes like the Greek ouzo, although it would not have been polite to say that. Considerable national pride often resides in the native drink of one's homeland. Malcolm told them his was the best, Arak Kawar. Those who stayed said he ended the slide show right after we left, and that's when the party really began. No one left till after two, someone said. We were not invited back.

Not many years later I heard Malcolm, Malachi, had returned to Israel to raise his family. He and his wife Miriam (named after the Old Testament prophetess who was the older sister of Moses and Aaron—yes, it was she who hid baby Moses in the bulrushes) had three kids, two girls and a boy, and she did not want to raise them in America. I understand he was teaching. I'd lost track of him, of course. It seems I'm good at doing that. I heard two stories: one that he'd been killed in a bombing, another that he'd died quite young and unexpectedly of a heart attack right there on the campus of Tel Aviv University. I think he wrote his dissertation on Mark Twain's *The Innocents Abroad*. Or maybe that's too appropriate to be true. Maybe he wrote his dissertation on Twain's next book, *Roughing It,* which concerns not the Holy Land, but my part of the world, a much more secular place.

Maybe this entire essay has been a digression. Maybe the real subject has to do with my inability to read premise fiction, fantasy, sci-fi, cyberpunk, whatever. Troublesome quotidian, mere reality, the plain old ordinary past with all of its fractured memories keeps getting in the way. The unusual piece I was reading ends with a couple of boys "celebrating." That's the last word in the story: "celebrating," as opposed to that other last word. I keep wondering about Malcolm and Miriam's kids, what's become of them. I'll bet they're really nice and kind and happy.

Timothy Murphy

Ode to Ford

> *Nel mezzo del cammin di nostra vita . . .*
> —*La Divina Commedia*, Dante Alighieri

I.
We'd had nearly two feet of snow
  and then the gale began to blow,
    gusting to thirty-five.
My charge? To carry to my mom's, alive
      and not to Hades,
        two ladies in their eighties.

  I never carried a heavier load.
  The lone vehicles on the road
    were Fords bigger than mine,
      and Fords? I have owned nine,
    little buggers, small SUV's
for fording streams and rounding fallen trees.

  Unplowed streets were blocked by buried cars,
  but it was Christmas, and my fortunate stars
    carried my fragile cargo
    from Moorhead clear to Fargo,
    over the river and through the wood,
and round the groaning board those ladies stood.
    Thank God for Ford.

II.

    The Bronco put-puts and dies,
    and the callow driver sighs,
a young man going nowhere in a hurry
  ten miles northwest of the Missouri.
    No water, money or hope,
  only a gentle, descending slope.

    His fuel filter is shot.
    He knows it is his fault, not
    the fault of his trusty Ford
whose scheduled service needs he has ignored.
  He muscles the red four-wheeler
  into motion and rolls to the dealer.

    This happened long ago
  in blazing heat, not blowing snow.
Grinning, an old mechanic watered the pup.
  Signing an IOU he was up
  and running. Customer loyalty?
  Try treating the poor like royalty.
    Thank God for Ford.

III.

Young man in camo, miles from any town:
  he didn't try to flag us down.
  Covered in mud, he looked half drowned,
  and I said, "Steve, let's turn around."
  "Yessir, I seem to have gotten stuck
  in my Chevy heavy-duty truck."

We drove down a dead-end lane
only the out-of-state would try in rain
    to a swamp no kid should be in.
    The two-ton truck was up to its chin
    in loon doo and mallard muck,
        but its driver was in luck.

Steve's F-150 and fifty feet of chain
pulled him from that greasy, bottomless drain
    my map marks as a road.
        Oh what a load!
And what a path in middle age we tread.
Syrdal declined the kid's money and said:
        Thank God for Ford.

N.S. Thompson

"Touched by the Light of the Real": A Note on Metaphor in the Poetry of B.H. Fairchild

And you will always need [tropes] because you hunger always for things seen in the light of everything else, and the light is endless
— "The Memory Palace"

Thought is the mind minding, poetry the mind embodied
—"Wittgenstein, Dying"

METAPHOR IS A RHETORICAL TROPE that helps to make a description or an image vivid in the mind of the reader or listener. Most usually it takes the form of a comparison: A is like B, where—from I.A. Richards (1937) onwards—the referent A is called the tenor and the comparison B is known as the vehicle. Alternative terms are "ground" (tenor) and "figure" (vehicle). Usually, in its simplest form, the comparison is made on the basis of commonly held identities. In saying that Hercules or other heroic figure from mythology possessed a lion's strength it is taken as read that the reader knows that the lion is a byword for strength and ferocity. If the reader happens not to know what a lion is, then the aim of the metaphor is thwarted. In this case, the metaphor also works by being succinct. It will be understood that—again assuming a common ground of knowledge—that there is no need to mention the strength of a lion, so we can simply say that, in battle, Hercules was a lion. The combined image of Hercules and the lion is compact and vivid, especially if we have seen a lion in action. Obviously Hercules is not

29

a lion, but in literature (and in everyday speech) it is understood that the statement is one of similarity, not perfect identity.

But literature often wants to go beyond the obvious and is keen not to fall into the well-worn paths of cliché. If we want vividness, then we continually have to be inventive. Thus we find that metaphors are often made between strikingly different areas of knowledge, experience or concept. It is also now recognized that metaphors are almost endemic in language and are not simply a rhetorical ornament. Nevertheless, they have been treated as such, although this will most likely change the more linguistic thought filters down. If they are explicatory rather than ornamental this is perhaps best illustrated when the literature happens to be mythological or, in some way, dealing with a world that is beyond this present world.

In the *Inferno* Dante had the brilliant idea of comparing what his persona saw there with observable sights on earth, thus rendering the imagined world both vivid and believable, but also—in a sinister way—metaphysically connected with this world. In Canto III the souls of the damned are figured as dead leaves falling off a tree until the personified branch sees them all littering the ground (ll. 112–114). Elsewhere in Canto XXIV, the poet's momentary despondency in Circle 8 is likened to that of the poor peasant in winter who despairs of finding food for his sheep (ll. 1–18). Throughout the entire journey through hell the reader is constantly reminded of the real world in the imagined one. When Dante and Virgil find the gates of Dis closed against them in Canto IX, an angel comes to open them and at its sight the fallen angels there disappear in a hurry as frogs do from their natural enemy, the snake, and dive in desperation to the bottom of the pond. There are many such examples in the great *cantico* and if gathered together would present a vivid picture of fourteenth century rural Tuscany.

Milton had a similar task in *Paradise Lost*. Perhaps taking his cue from Dante, the fallen angels in Book I are described as lying thick as the autumnal leaves in Vallombrosa (ll. 301–304). It helps to know that the Italian name means "shady valley" with the sinister connotations of darkness. Several lines earlier Satan had been described in heroic terms with his shield hanging like the moon seen from Fiesole through an "optic glass" (Galileo's telescope), his spear equal to "the tallest pine/ Hewn on Norwegian hills" (ll. 292–293) for the mast of some great admiral's ship. The imaginary is made vivid by reference to reality.

On the other hand, a writer can make the metaphor into a puzzle that the reader has to solve, combining very disparate elements to create the metaphor. Why should they choose to do this? It may afford the writer the opportunity to explain the connection and reveal that as an epiphany, or they can choose to let the reader work out the connection and hope the epiphany will reveal itself. In "A Valediction: Forbidding Mourning," John Donne wished his readers to understand a pair of lovers as being like a pair of compasses. A pair of thin pointed pieces of metal? Are they sharp and cold lovers? No, one is a fixed point to which the other will always return after necessary travel. A farfetched analogy, perhaps, and one that has no obvious connection, but rather is an explicable one through analysis of that perceived connection, which Donne provides. This kind of metaphor is called a conceit, after the Italian "*concetto*" (concept, thought). Here the metaphorical is not so much visual as conceptual.

Given the above highly condensed and partial—but I hope sufficient—introduction to metaphor, it is interesting to turn to a contemporary poet who is very much in the American grain of realism, often relating scenes and images from his own life and yet hungers to communicate "in the light of everything else." As ever, any writer wants to avoid clichés and make the work vivid for the reader. This inevitably means thinking up new analogies, and for that there is no limit except what an audience will accept. You may think that the landscapes of rural Midwest America are not the best or most exciting scenery to have to evoke in vivid terms. Moreover, in what terms do you see the landscape and its objects? Is there any need to see them differently in some or any way?

It depends on what a poet is trying to do. If satire, then the field is wide open. There are enough foolish and extravagant aspects of life from which the writer can choose to make connections. Cartoonists are especially good at creating visual analogies here. But what if, like Wordsworth, the poet wishes to see into the very heart of things; wants indeed to share with the reader a special moment when vision does seem transcendent and we see far more than our optical senses? We may wish to communicate any amount of emotion in the image(s) before us, especially sympathy or compassion, or even simply with an innocence that helps communicate an untrammeled view. Metaphors can also be a persuasive means to look inside the poet's head and understand the vision, precisely "the mind embodied."

A look through B.H. Fairchild's *The Blue Buick: New and Selected Poems* (W.W. Norton, 2014), a selection taken from the five volumes of poetry he has written over thirty years, together with new poems, gives many striking examples of what can be done when the poet cleverly combines like with like in one sense (the metaphor or simile), but also the very unlike in others (the conceit). One might call this metaphorical link multi-stranded, multivalent or, in old-fashioned literary terms, simply ambiguous—but fruitfully and meaningfully so.

What is striking is that seldom does the poet need recourse to a different conceptual world. The vehicles most often come from the very same semantic plane as the tenors, so that reality ends up reinforcing and enhancing reality. Rarely does the poet step outside this model.

The first line of the first poem gives an indication of what is to come. In "The Woman at the Laundromat Crying 'Mercy'" the dryers are seen as "glass eyes" that "whirl." On the level of reality, it is the inside of the dryers that whirl as the drum rotates, whereas the poet is making a connection between the circularity of eyes with the unsaid addition of lenses, together with the action of the letting the eyes roll in surprise or wonder. Here the image is a way for the poem to express surprise at the minor tragedies that occur in the laundromat, such as the variety of moral and immoral messages on the notice board, the change machine jamming and the woman crying "*mercy, mercy.*" At the centre of the poem the "Long white rows of washers lead/ straight as highways to a change machine." This last line is again more of a conceit than a standard metaphor (if we can actually define such a thing). Long white rows of washers are not like highways. And who says highways are straight? We have to position ourselves in the rural Midwest, where they are very straight indeed. But it is the associations that are crucial here, the orderliness, the idea of leading somewhere, even the cleanness. What is also crucial is that both tenor and vehicle (washers and highways) come from the same visual landscape, as it were, yet from completely unexpected parts of it. In the same way, a glass eye is part of the same lived reality as a drying machine, if a less common element.

In "The Men," the character Billy is "slumped over/ his beer like a snail," which is more like a Dantesque association except that the tenor is from the world of observable reality, unlike the dead souls in the *Inferno*. But the rich associations of snail go beyond the hunched or humped shape seen in the human image. There is the protective shell and the soft vulnerable creature inside. Later in the same poem the poet's persona is "feeling young and strong enough to raise/ the sun back up," a very striking and original image which seems to coalesce an Atlas-like quality of uplift with the domestic act of rolling up a blind or raising up a picture fallen from a wall. The connection here would be the unsaid ease with which the action is envisaged. It is part of the observable world, just like raising a picture.

Indeed it is in the realm of the pictorial that Fairchild is most vivid, his visual metaphors (the vehicles) are not a million miles from the thing to be described and yet are so fresh and unexpected. It is the very closeness of the tenor and vehicle in their everyday reality, and yet the unexpected yoking together, that is so suggestive and compelling, because there is also a distance between the two. Perhaps it could be expected to see "silver dirigibles move[d] like great whales" in "Flight," but in "Angels" a patient has a "head wrapped like a gift" and the nurses have "white dresses puffed out like pigeons/ in the morning breeze." The first image reinforces the gift of health offered by the dressing, and the nurses' dresses bring to mind the promise of a new day as heralded by the birds cooing. The poem "Hair" describes a barber's shop and the "white cotton cloths/ that drape [men's] bodies like little nightgowns./ How like well-behaved children they seem—" and moves on to the man who sits with a "razor humming small hymns along his neck." The associations of innocence and sanctity (and perhaps vulnerability) taken from the everyday world contrast with the macho image the men wish to project. Again, what is compelling is the nearness in terms of domestic reality, and yet also the distance from the men's tough-guy aspirations.

As one moves through the collection, the poetry becomes less visual and more concerned with voice, especially that of the dramatic monologue. As mentioned above, it is well known among linguists that everyday speech is as colorful with metaphors as figurative poetry and yet Fairchild does not reflect this. Although a cliché, my young ears were thrilled to hear someone driving at speed described as "going like the clappers down the East Lancs Road." So it is not that a non-poetic voice would necessarily be devoid of metaphor, but this could reflect the language of the rural Midwest or, at least, Fairchild's experience or perception of it. Nevertheless in "The Soliloquy of the Appliance Repairman" the man sees himself figuratively as the savior of domestic appliances: a "healer and name-brand magician, [who] . . . must raise them from the dead." This, however, is about as far as metaphor and the figurative go with these personae and the later poetry is heavily populated with them, from the poet manqué Roy Eldridge Garcia to the student Nathan Gold, from the unfortunate freak-show exhibit Frieda Pushnik to Hart Crane.

It is in the detail of the poet's own personal experience that metaphor comes into its own, where he shows unequaled mastery in bringing his often felt youthful boredom and despair crisply alive, with a wonderful analogy that may come from left field but hits home perfectly. In "Maize" his parents experience "harvest like a huge wall" and in "In Another Life I Encounter My Father" a successful hit in baseball makes a "ball fat as a cantaloupe," but there are extended metaphors reminiscent of Milton (e.g., the prowling wolf and thief in *Paradise Lost,* IV, ll. 183–192), as in the poem "Cigarettes":

> my father,
> for instance, smoking L&M's all night in the kitchen,
> a sea of smoke risen to neck level as I wander in
> like some small craft drifting and lost in fog
> while a distant lighthouse flares awhile and swings away.

The metaphor of smoke as a "sea" leads on to the image of the child as a "small craft," and brilliantly to the image of the glowing cigarette end moving to and fro as being like the intermittent flashes of a lighthouse. Most important in this composite image is the metaphorical but also conceptual fog between father and son. It is a vivid and beautifully succinct image for "the despair of certain domestic scenes" the poem mentions.

The metaphors can be visual or auditory (e.g., laughter "rich as brass rivets rolling down a tin roof" in "Keats") working on the same planes of reality, but are most successful of all when the image conjures up a state of mind, what one could also term an objective correlative as described by Eliot[2]. Nevertheless, there is always a link with observable reality as here in his father's machine shop where "A shrill, sullen truculence blows in like dust

---

2 "[A] set of objects, a situation, a chain of events which shall be the formula of that particular emotion; such that when the external facts, which must terminate in sensory experience, are given, the emotion is immediately evoked." T.S. Eliot, "Hamlet and His Problems," in *The Sacred Wood,* 100.

devils" and in the case of "Boredom/ grows thick as maize in Kansas" ("Rave On"). The two terms are to be taken humorously and satirically—if also seriously—as synonymous. Elsewhere objects are seen as people, animals or birds and sounds and emotions are seen in terms of weather, with "Quiet as a first snow" ("The Beauty of Abandoned Towns") and "Happiness comes down like rain" ("The Left Fielder's Sestina").

Apart from what might be seen as the domestic referents detailed above, albeit skillfully used, Fairchild's poetry is not devoid of high culture reference (from jazz, ballet and visual art, to philosophy), which contrast starkly, but not unkindly, with his working class background and the boredom, "thick as maize in Kansas," from which he is eventually to escape. But his use of metaphor in describing his first world should be noted and commended for its imaginative use of what might be termed contiguous elements so near and yet so far away. Perhaps the effect is best summed up by lines from the middle of "All the People in Hopper's Paintings" where the poet refers to Edward Hopper's three paintings "Gas" (1940), "Nighthawks"(1942), and "Sea Watchers" (1952):

> But on the white island of the station,
> the luminous squares from its windows
> lying quietly like carpets on the pavement
> had been my hope, my sense of the real world
> beyond the familiar one, like the blazing café
> of the nighthawks casting the town into shadow,
> or the beach house of the sea watchers
> who sat suspended on a verandah of light,
> stunned by the flat, hard sea of the real.

As in Hopper's work, light is used to enhance reality and the light of metaphor as seen in Fairchild's work is endless in its enhancement of the real and the everyday, making it numinous and memorable.

Pedro Poitevin

Burial with a Storm

For Alejandro Glusman, voice of WHPK, Chicago

Today I need to bury you again.
Pick up a shovel, stomp its blade across
the edges of your noble resting place,
then dig until your coffin is in view.

Today I need a sacred hurricane.
I need to see the dust return to dust
and fly in threads of wind—escape this maze
of skyscrapers and houses, blow right through.

Today I need a storm to scatter bones.
Your skull should go to Israel at last.
Your hands should land with me in Marblehead.
Your vertebrae belong in Illinois.

Today I need to pick up all these stones,
return each one of them to sand or grass.
May radio waves now gather overhead
and let me hear the ripples of your voice.

Joseph Hutchison

Touch

. . . as though all life were death.
— Ferdowsi

I

"If all you have is a hammer, everything
looks like a nail." Say it: Implements speak.
Thus guns whisper to ruptured psyches: *Touch
me all over. Feel how I quiver with the fire
damped in us both. Hold me,* breathes the gun.
Trigger our one desire—and I will raise you up.

II

A street punk fucked my friend's son up
for his wallet and a thrill. *Pop-pop.* Everything
bled out: past, future, Furies, gods. The gun
barked, and the stars forgot how to speak,
and silence poured down on my friend like fire
as he reached out for what he could not touch.

III

Have bloody entertainments murdered touch?
Facebook bullying? Torture by proxy? Look up:
the sky that seems so empty is, in fact, on fire
with being. We imagine emptiness in everything
to break the shackles of desire, the longing to speak,
to *be.* Emptiness absolves as it thunders from the gun.

IV

Mailman, mailman, where's my gun? My gun,
my flex-tip ammo, my 30-round mags. (A touch
of manic cunning's trained him not to speak
such litanies out loud.) Who can say what's up?
Even the scheming shooter can't grasp everything
he aims to do; but he'll at last feel real when he fires.

V

As a kid I watched Davy Crockett by the campfire:
coonskin cap, possum stew, his muzzle-load long gun
propped against a Hollywood pine. How everything
glowed! How fondly the frontier king would touch
Old Betsy, slowly swab her barrel, then snatch her up
to kill some red marauder with nary a line to speak.

VI

They bleed in theaters, temples, schools; they speak
no more, love and dream no more. The same fire
kills them in cubicles, parking lots, alleys, up
in the boardroom, down in the lobby. Only the gun
doesn't bleed, exists to penetrate what it won't touch,
what the shooter won't touch—which is everything.

VII

Touch matters. Say it! Tears well up in everything.
Touch them. Stroke skin, not steel. In the mirror, touch
the Other's face—a fire that will never speak from a gun.

You Mock Me

You mock me, little brat.
If I had a head as hot
as the fire under your coat
I'd have no need of a hat
any more than a feeble sot
needs a coat to warm his fat.

That coal you thought was black
is burning up in your sac,
where it's hotter than any ember.
But a covered fire will blaze,
smokier, higher, wilder,
and longer than you'll remember.

My head was frozen stiff
and my brain a cracked hieroglyph
when I emptied them into this mule
for four years straight, like a fool,
and wanting to beat him dead,
I beat myself instead.

And that crazy sapper hick
pulled up at the wrong pile of brick
at the wrong turn in the road
so rattled and lost, his load
of crude explosives got shaken
and blew his brains to bacon.

> — *Translated from the French[3] of Pierre de Ronsard*
> *by Terese Coe*

---

3   See "Translation Notes" on page 134 for the original French poem.

Shadow Kisses

Shadow kisses, shadow love,
shadow life, how cool!
Do you imagine they will be
unchanged forever, fool?

Our every fond obsession,
like dream, will discompose,
and soon the heart and mind forget,
and soon the eyelids close.

*— Translated from the German[4] of Heinrich Heine
by Terese Coe*

---

[4]   See "Translation Notes" on page 135 for the original German poem.

Rachel Hadas

Dandelion Fluff

Boxes packed to send back to the past.
Antagonists eyeball their enemies.
Damp green trees, mosquitoes, mountains, clouds:
has a resolution come at last?

Where do mountains end and clouds begin?
Stuffed shelves and winding stair
deferred; the years of clutter overnight
melted into morning. Here we are.

Make sense of them—the endless spectral layers,
warp and woof through which we pick our way.
A little girl blows dandelion fluff.
Precipice. Diagnosis. Augury.

Brunch at Bread & Ink

In memory of Ken Arnold[5], 1944–2014

Brunch at Bread & Ink. November noon.
Unfathomable change is coming. Soon?

Death: a door. But how to say goodbye?
Your face is calm, not valedictory.

Our looks across the table take and give.
No one can say how long they have to live.

Late loves hover. Better not to seek
precise predictions year or month or week.

The greeting in this gathering is Hello.
I still have a lot of inner work to do.

A week of silence: *opportunity*
to go deeper into this mystery.

Brunch at Bread & Ink, a sunlit portal
through which five friends pass, none of us immortal.

---

5   See author's notes on page 141.

Stephen Palos

Lineage

We did not remove our shoes. My father followed
a dirty trail from the doorway to the love seat
where Grandpa sat and smoked, a little glass
of milk perched on the table at his side.

Above him, fruit flies stuck to a strip of tape
like small black seeds. My father moved a pillow
and sat beside the man I'd only known
from blurred photos and stories.
                              When we hugged,
his trembling arms reached out like shepherd crooks
and pulled me down. He coughed into my ear,
apologized, and looked me in the eyes.

He stared at me, then frowned. His lips were thin,
dried peppers, wording something. Flecks of milk
clung to his beard. I pulled myself away
and asked my father where the restroom was.

He nodded toward the hall. Two figurines,
naked, kneeled atop the toilet tank.
The room stank of hay, damp—I didn't touch
the humid toilet handle.
                              When I returned,
they didn't notice. Keeping back, I watched
my father pull a comb through his father's hair,
starting at the ends and working up.

Stephen Palos

Lost in the Supermarket

Walk without comfort, little wanderer,
and cry your tears to the margins. Go behind
the well-walls of your eyelids, where you grope
for rungs in darkness. That is not your mother,
talking ceaselessly into a phone, and
that is not your mother, staring at her reflection
in a window, pulling her shirt to better cover
her not-your-mother breasts. You have searched
beneath a pop machine on hands and knees,
but found no map to her location, no ticket
to hand an usher for a glimpse. She walks
in parking lots, by lakesides, on the metro,
but always she is moving farther and farther
from you. She is home now. She is going to bed.
She is dreaming away your face, your voice, your name,
believing you will lose sight of her as well.

Andrew Valentine

Medals

IT WAS ONE OF THOSE THINGS. Seabass said he'd jump The Bluff and we both agreed to do it too. We didn't know how high it was. Freaky high from what we'd heard. Apparently Fuller's cousin had jumped it and hit the water at such an angle that all the chemicals stored in her spine came loose and sent her into a trip. We thought we were men, is what it came down to. Seabass liked to chew tobacco. He stole his dad's Skoal and lugged it around in a Ziploc bag. By the time we made it into the woods and smoked a bowl and opened the bag, the chew was dry and smelled the way our bookshelf smelled since Mom used to read her books in the bath.

Seabass was a moocher too. He'd always hit me up for a buck when we went to the Burger King out by the freeway. Years later, I heard he got rich selling dishwasher parts.

Lake Oswego was a town of hills, and everything sloped toward the water. When they drained the lake on certain years, the town would reek of sewage and mud. You could venture down and walk through the waste where people had dropped things out of their boats. Seabass found a Goldschläger label. I dug up a silver watch. The gears were stuck and the face had clouded, but under the fog you could make out the time. The exact second everything stopped.

Late summer, when Seabass said he'd jump The Bluff, the water was high on the limestone banks and the algae bloom had already come and the breeze carried waves of sulphuric rot like compost containers left in the sun. The Bluff rose out of the western bank, facing east where the algae was thickest. The only access up to the top was a narrow street named Phantom Court—two or three homes set back from the sidewalk, dense ferns in the yards. The road rose sharply and met its end at the edge of the trees. We had to stand on a transformer box in order to hurdle the chain-link fence. In the lowest branches, some of the leaves

44

were starting to turn. The ivy was thick with cobwebs and thorns.

We'd smoked already. Seabass was sucking his dried-out Skoal. Fuller had eaten some liberty caps. I remember his face as we left the brush, the uneasy pressure that clouded his eyes. We'd made it now to the top of The Bluff and the only obvious way down was to jump. It had to be at least ninety feet. We crept to the edge and tried to gauge how fast we would fall. The lake didn't look like a lake anymore. The surface seemed like solid ground.

Along to our right we discovered the ledge where Fuller's cousin was meant to have jumped. It extended from the cliff like a diving platform. Seabass hawked one over the side and we watched his saliva waver in the breeze and then disappear.

"Damn," he said. "That shit is high." He dropped his backpack onto the rocks, took off his T-shirt, walked to the edge with his hands on his hips.

"Too high," Fuller said. "Way too high."

Seabass raised his eyebrows at me. "See, Nate? I told you he'd bitch."

One of Fuller's pupils dilated. Seabass stood looking out at the lake with all the boat docks spoking its rim, the boats themselves just varying blobs, and the Kelok Bridge a strip in the distance. I can't imagine what he was thinking. I was dreaming of paper maps. Tracing a route to the edge of the world. Sudden endings. I blinked the wetness out of my eyes. Seabass had removed his sneakers. His jeans were laid out over a rock. He lined up for a running start.

"Maybe we shouldn't do this," I said.

Seabass rolled his eyes. "If Fuller's cousin can jump this thing . . ." he paused, sniffed, spit out his chew. "Look, man. I need to ask you something important."

"Alright."

"Okay. Don't lie. I'll know if you lie."

"Fine. What is it?"

"Are you a bitch?"

I stared directly into his eyes.

"Say it," he said. "Say you're not a frightened bitch."

Then he sprinted over the side. I counted the seconds. The splash was only a muffled hiss. Fuller and I peeked down at the water. Seabass emerged and slapped the surface, breaking holes in the algae around him. We watched him swim toward the middle.

"Nate!" he called. "Naaaa-aaaate! Come on, bitches!"

Fuller had gone into breathing fits. He cradled his head and back-stepped away. I think the truth was sinking in. If I jumped next he *had* to jump, otherwise Seabass would never shut up. The whole school would know. Any person with functioning ears. Fuller the bitch, Fuller the bitch. Worst of all, the story would reach Samantha Balk. Tall, beautiful soccer-team Balk, molecules dancing wherever she walked.

I stripped to my boxers and heaped my clothes on top of a shrub. Fuller stood there looking at me. He opened his mouth but nothing came out. The ground was vibrating. Maybe my knees were starting to shake. I remembered Newton's first law of motion, the trust exercises we studied in Physics.

"Dude," Fuller finally croaked. "I'm coming up way too fast."

I didn't have time to respond. I felt the way you feel in a plane. The takeoff. How the ground drops away and something jolts in the pit of your gut and you can't make out what you're seeing below. A motionless, visceral blur of shapes. The only thing holding you up is yourself, and the air. Then the descent down two-hundred stories, the wall of The Bluff whipping wind at my back and the water approaching and sucking me in. Silence. Darkness. The echoing thrum of bubbles rising, tendrils of algae slick on my thighs. I breached the surface and swam toward Seabass, who had his arms raised over his head. He clapped me on the scalp and smiled.

"I knew it," he said.

I turned around. The Bluff looked fake. A headstone rising out of a puddle. I thought somehow my eyes had shrunk, or come dislodged when I entered the water and floated away to the eastern bank. Then I noticed the ledge up top, Fuller standing there shirtless and pale. He looked like a toothpick stuck in a wedge. Seabass tapped the top of his wrist, gazing expectantly up at our friend. Fuller stepped backwards, out of sight. A few seconds passed before he returned.

"Oh, fuck you!" Seabass yelled. "Dude, just do it!"

Fuller disappeared again. While he was gone, I became aware that time had stopped.

When life accelerates out of a standstill, the moments pass as a series of frames. You can actively watch the clock gain speed. Fuller arrived sprinting slow-motion. He reached the ledge and hesitated. A single frame of indecision. His foot slipped. I'd seen footage of divers missing their marks

and clacking their heads on the lip of the springboard. When Fuller fell backwards, everything filtered into bronze. The back of his skull met the rock at full-speed. A burst of blood like mist from a blowhole. He hit the lake horizontally and reemerged limp, floating face-down. His limbs were spread in the shape of a star.

We used our voices. Screaming, mostly. The Lake Patrol boated us back to shore. CPR was performed on the bank. We were questioned briefly by a man with a mustache. His partner, a woman with deep-set eyes, called for an ambulance. Then the lights took Fuller away, leaving me and Seabass behind.

We hiked silently back to the top. There were thorns in the webbing between my toes by the time we reached the ledge again. I leaned on a rock and brushed my soles and pulled the barbs from my skin.

Seabass shoved a dip in his gum. "How are you getting home?" he said. "I think I'm gonna call my dad."

There were tears in my eyes.

Seabass spit and shook his head. "You're a bitch sometimes, you know that, Nate?"

"Don't call me that."

"Hey, man." He spit again. "I calls it like I sees it."

I was standing. I marched toward Seabass and shoved him, hard. He hit the ground with a choking sound and rearranged to his hands and knees, gagging and heaving.

"Fuck, man! I swallowed my chew! Ah, shit!"

I stood over him, arms folded. "You're nuts, Seabass. Didn't you hear the EMT? Fuller's gonna have *brain damage*, dude."

"Fuck Fuller," he choked. "Fuller's a bitch."

An anvil dropped and squashed my heart. I walked to the treeline and slumped to my knees and sobbed. I heard Seabass vomit. After a time, things went quiet. Only the sound of the wind in the trees and the lap of the lake at the base of The Bluff. I felt Seabass kneel beside me.

"You wanna smoke a bowl?" he asked. "I got some here."

I looked at the pipe and shook my head. "Today was fucking stupid," I said. "I can't believe you thought this would work. That this would be a good idea." It struck me that I was speaking to myself as much as I was speaking to him. "Such a dumbass," I breathed at last.

Seabass didn't feel like me. He hurled the pipe into the trees, pushed me flat and pinned me down.

"What did you say?" he said. "You little bitch. Just because *your* house is lined with books and mine smells like a fucking ashtray. Just because your perfect life is better than mine, motherfucker, doesn't mean you can call me dumb. If you're so smart, why are you here with me right now?"

I watched the clouds turn overhead. The sky was tinged with silver streaks. Seabass spit and leaned in close. I felt his breath inside my nose.

"You're not like me, Nate. I don't always win these games."

Then he hurried into the brush. I heard the fence rattle. After that I was on my own. I dressed quickly and checked my phone. I called my house, but no one answered. Dad was out again.

The whole way home I thought about Seabass. His parents owned a failing thrift store and rarely went to work anymore. That's how Seabass said it was. I caught myself feeling guilty. I saw him curled on a secondhand mattress. The used up things inside their house, the fraying armchairs and hand-me-down clothes and chipped plates and glasses and the fullscreen TV. I remembered the car his father drove. A gold Impala from the 1980s with a dent the size of a fist in its hood. They were speeding home in that vehicle now. Engine roaring, windows down. I stopped for breath and peered up the street. Another hill was waiting for me, and this was the steepest road in town.

Barbara Haas

Resurrection Kaleidoscope

LASHED BY RAIN AND VEXED by an UMBRELLA that kept turning itself inside out, I dashed across the wet cobbles alongside the Griboyedov Canal and ducked into the Resurrection Cathedral on Spilled Blood. This close to the Gulf of Finland, capricious summer storms assailed Saint Petersburg willy-nilly every afternoon, often dumping an inch of precipitation in a slanted torrent before all at once breaking to reveal a sky of the most intense bluebird hue. Dinner was more than two hours away, and my intention had been to spend that time leisurely browsing through Dom Knigi, the House of Books on Nevsky Prospekt. I liked stocking up on exotic editions of Dostoevski, Tolstoy and Chekhov every summer before heading back to the States. Today I had made it halfway there when the heavens opened up, so I sought refuge in this onion dome cathedral along the canal.

A handful of people were milling about in the dim antechamber, some folding up umbrellas and giving them to the coat check babushka, others examining a brochure about the decorative mosaics inside the sanctuary. The Resurrection Cathedral was the most dramatic landmark in Saint Petersburg, a tour de force example of over-the-top architecture in the highly ornate, cupola-bedecked bulbous Russian style.

The dimness of this antechamber mimicked the gloom outside. The musty scent of wet stone rose around us. Heavy wooden doors led to the sanctuary, and small tour groups huddled before them with their guides. I saw glimmering through the gap where two doors met a seam of white light. When people passed through and went inside, a full-wattage brilliance engulfed them. This light did not spill into the murk where we stood or illuminate the antechamber in any way but stayed very contained, very sequestered in the sanctuary, as if to cross that threshold back toward us, to leave its post and pass through those doors, were somehow out of the question. The light flared, it radiated, but it remained neatly held within. Even when the doors were closed and all I could see was that thin bright stripe, I nonetheless had the sense of the light concentrating its energy, confining and consolidating it. This was a light that would not come to you. You had to go to it. I had visited Saint Petersburg four times and had never set foot inside its most illustrious building.

A young man standing next to me—maybe he was my son's age—pointed to a Cyrillic phrase in the brochure he was holding and in British-accented English asked me to translate. He had a soft new beard, fine threads and silky wisps curving against an angular jaw, like a man's first beard though he was perhaps twenty-three or twenty-four years old. He possessed the demeanor of an intellectual, eyes deep-set—still and unblinking. There was something cerebral and intent in his gaze. I looked at the phrase he was showing me in the brochure: на крови.

"On blood," I said.

He cut me a side glance and nodded a sheepish assent, as if to say, "Well, of course," a private smile quirking the edge of his mouth. After all, this was the Cathedral *on Spilled Blood*. Petersburgers were so casual they dropped "Resurrection" entirely and just called it Spilled Blood. A tour group moved toward the heavy twin doors. Tucking the brochure into his back pocket, he joined them. The doors cracked open, and the sanctuary blazed with a white intensity. Everything seemed to vanish in the white burn.

на крови.

The cathedral had been built on the exact spot where an assassin's bomb cut down Alexander II in 1881. Although the perpetrator, an anti-monarchist radical, was apprehended immediately, the residents of Saint Petersburg were themselves blamed for the heinous act. Their sin? Not Russian enough. Too European, too western.

So European that they had failed to thwart regicidal mayhem in their midst.

Un-Russian. Unable to keep their divine leader safe.

The people were made to foot the bill for this cathedral "to enshrine the blood of the assassinated tsar," this according to historian Richard Wortman in his essay "The Russian Style in Church Architecture." The building itself would be "an act of repentance for [embracing] Western culture."

It was true that since its founding Saint Petersburg had looked European, its art and architecture boldly neoclassical, hailing from Italian, Dutch, French and Prussian masters. This was Peter the Great's extravagant Window on the West, meant to bring the world cascading voluptuously in, one luscious baroque wave after another. Fountains were designed to out-Versailles Versailles, churches to rival the masterpieces of Rome and Paris—harmonious, balanced, symmetrical, restrained. The cityscape was a builder's playground: confection after architectural confection in peach tones, butter yellow and mint. Saint Petersburg was a European intoxication in the heart of Imperial Russia. Tuscan porticoes were resplendent with columns, rooflines squared to Bavarian design.

Had the city kept its window open too long?

In 1881 the bloodstain of the Tsar stood as an indictment of this degenerate failing. "Alien, Western influences were to be dispelled; the capital was to be resanctified by making it more like Moscow," according to Wortman. The Resurrection Cathedral would be the atonement—On Spilled Blood. Its exterior would hearken back to the medieval ecclesiastic style of earlier centuries, with St. Basil's on Red Square as the perfect model. It would be a riot of blooming *kokoshniki* petals unfurling from flamboyant tent-shaped steeples, all of it ornamented to excess with *girki* (limestone pendants) and *shirinki* (deeply recessed enamel squares). Where Ivan the Terrible had intended St. Basil's as the new Jerusalem in 1561, this cathedral more than three centuries later would have an intention, too: "to administer an open rebuke to the city and constitute an effort to Muscovitize Saint Petersburg."

Here I stood in the elaborate rebuke.

How much guilt could one cathedral redeem? How much atonement would be enough?

The light of the sanctuary slanted piercingly between the heavy doors, just a thread, a micron, a stripe. Periodically Russia had to recolonize itself. It had to reclaim its look, its feel, its story. Sometimes it threw open its window on the world . . . Other times it slammed the thing adamantly shut.

I thought of the way the US had practiced "shock Capitalism" with the former Soviet economy after the collapse of the USSR. In 1992 a team of Harvard economists showed up in Moscow ready to school the Russians on how to privatize state property, create a new business elite and grow the middle class.

That open window . . . So tempting.

More recently the world had seen a coup in Ukraine—practically on Russia's doorstep—and then the annexing of Crimea

just after. Even before the West had come down hard with tough financial sanctions, Russia was withdrawing, pulling into itself, becoming more nationalistic, more militaristic, embracing the Motherland, embracing the Fatherland, finding comfort in its conservative Orthodox Christianity, getting nostalgic about the hammer and sickle. Periodically, Russia had to step back, go within itself, had to remember who it was.

Just a thread, a micron, a stripe.

This was one of those periods.

The seam between the heavy doors shone candescent white, and when a small tour group pushed through to go inside, I followed.

Towering arches, vaulted ceilings, high chapels and altars, every surface encrusted with rare stones and gems. Gold paint, gold enamel, gold chandeliers suspended like brilliant clouds of spun gold from sparkling gold chains, their golden candelabra glowing gold against pillars resplendent with gold leaf embedded in glass. The eye found no rest here. This sanctuary was a Hallelujah Chorus of dynamic winking color in quarter-inch tiles and tiny cubes of cut malachite, lapis lazuli, tiger eye. Pebbles of amber backed by bronze-tinted mirrors studded the length of floor-to-ceiling pilasters. The sheer density of décor made it seem like resurrection had never existed anywhere on earth before Russia invented it right here right on the spot. Polished slabs of porphyry, anthracite, green serpentine and picture jasper framed mosaics dedicated to the risen Christ.

Russia was effusive and big. It never did anything small—whether mounting revolutions, building cities in swamps, oppressing its people or defeating an enemy. In the US we often overlook or fail to recognize how forged in faith a country like Russia actually is. American history has no corollary to a tsar, for instance, no way of comprehending a leader who is the earthly manifestation of God. Mormonism could offer an example of this, as could Catholicism in its obedience to the Pope, but neither religious branch dominates our democracy or issues forth laws. Indeed, when JFK was campaigning for president in 1960 and his Catholicism raised concerns, he addressed the issue forcefully—"I believe in an America where the separation of Church and State is absolute"—in effect paraphrasing Thomas Jefferson.

Beginning especially with Ivan the Terrible in the mid-1500s Russian monuments and churches were built to reinforce the autocrat's special relationship to the deity, declaratory architecture in a sense: brick and stone testimony to the will of divine providence in the person of the tsar. A full two centuries before the American Constitution, Moscow was already conceiving of itself as the New Jerusalem. The gold-painted frescoes gracing the thick inner walls of heavily fortified cathedrals were already transposing the Jesus narrative to Russia, were removing Rome, removing Byzantium, removing any foreign claim on Christianity and impressing upon the people a new state mythology: Russia as the site of Christ's story.

So the assassination of Alexander II in 1881 was not only a blow of geopolitical magnitude but also an unspeakable assault on Russian spiritual identity.

When our country suffered the assassinations of beloved presidents—Lincoln, Kennedy—our American inclination never to mix the religious with the political kept the shock at a manageably secular level. Not to say that these atrocities weren't calamitous—they were. We grieved the human loss of leadership, of course—the Father of our country!—and mourned the national potential lost in that leadership. Building the Lincoln Memorial in DC became our own special American sort of declaration of this—also the Eternal Flame in Arlington Cemetery to mark Kennedy's grave.

Something told me that those things would not have been enough for Russia.

My gaze climbed an entablature of crimson granite whose dark veins of manganese braided a path all the way to the cathedral's high arching dome, where the raised hand of Christ the Redeemer bestowed a blessing on all of us down here below. A firmament of stars glimmered around him, backed by celestial bodies. When Russia demanded atonement, it went so far over the top you could see the aurora borealis. And when Russia did resurrection it omitted nothing.

I moved close to a mosaic of St. Alexander Nevsky and saw each cubed tessara nestled against the tessara beside it, a bead of grout joining them. I moved back and saw how every hand-placed piece vanished into the overall panorama. One by one, row by row, the individual cubes, though numerous, were devoid of nuance or content if singled out or scrutinized alone and studied by themselves. Resurrection would not happen here in one concussive blow but bit by bit, shard by inlaid shard—each piece inert, carrying no particular charge, like nitric acid kept far from glycerin, but igniting its meaning only when combined with the others.

A dozen tesserae formed a subtle gradient from turquoise to teal in a wall mosaic of the

Ascension, and I leaned in to examine the exact quarter-inch piece where the color shift happened. I moved back. I moved close. We were all doing that. Back and forth, back and forth, like breathing in and out, in and out— as if we were a single organism, inhaling, exhaling, a giant lung. The concentration of imagery was uniting us—breathing, breathing—not many lives but one.

The color began to swim before my eyes, and I sat down on an alabaster bench. Some people were lighting candles, some crossing themselves repeatedly, some snapping selfies—Christ and I. Some had tears in their eyes. People swayed in place, heads thrown back, staring up at the dome of heaven. They, too, were the individual pieces in a living mosaic that formed and reshuffled in this cathedral.

Saints and martyrs peered out from arches, doorframes and inner curves. Every surface featured a prophet or angel, watchful guardians posting up. Panel after mosaic panel emphasized the high points in the resurrection narrative: Christ on the road to Emmaus, Christ in the upper room, Christ by the Sea of Galilee. Columns were beveled inward at each corner, flat spaces that made more area for imagery, more room for resurrection. Even an atheist could not escape the narrative fusillade. It would not convert you so much as conquer you. The aggressive insistence on this unswerving story transcended religion, ironically enough. It was pervasive, overpowering, a total take down. The cathedral seemed to release its resurrection in shrapnel fragments, quarter-inch by quarter-inch, all of it packed in tightly and ready to detonate in a blast of divine light.

I found myself blinking furiously and staring down at my feet. The floor was an assemblage of cut marble—fourteen different types and colors—in intricate star-shaped patterns and boxy parallelograms. When the Bolsheviks seized control in 1917, the cathedral became the Ministry of the People's Will, a place devoted, incredibly enough, to worshipping and lauding the very assassination it had been built to redeem. In the 1930s Stalin shut it down, fearing his own assassination, and there were plans to implode it. But during the Siege of Leningrad the building was needed as a cold-storage morgue for the citizens who died of starvation until a mass gravesite could be prepared, and the Resurrection Cathedral on Spilled Blood became a temporary tomb.

I tried to imagine the linen-shrouded bodies laid beside each other and pushed up against these ornate walls, orderly rows stacked higher and higher, body after body, each one of them a white piece in a tragic mosaic that rose to a wretched revelation— seven thousand dead on Christmas Day, 1941; five thousand the day after. From all over the city, families pulled their lost loved ones on sleds through the snow, and workers stacked the bodies. Even in the dim light of a Leningrad winter the blank whiteness of death would contradict the fiery color of resurrection here. I tried to imagine the mute companionship of these sentry figures overseeing that scene from their framed panels on the posts and pillars—the placid and timeless gaze of St. Gleb, himself a martyr, untroubled as he looked down on the shrouded forms below. Next to him, from a pulpit of mosaic feldspar, and with an expression of one who has relinquished all earthly care, St. Boris surveyed that congregation of death.

How much blood? How much heaven?

One Resurrection Cathedral was all it took to redeem Saint Petersburg. There were no other buildings like this here. When Russia recolonized itself it did so in one strategic blast. No need to repeat the message on other streets or along other canals or in a showy plaza somewhere. Once was enough. This was declaratory architecture at its finest, a powerscape in one structure, an across-the-bow statement straight from the autocrat. And Russia made a statement, it did not stutter.

Tour groups were breaking up, and people scattering back outside into a late afternoon brilliance that sparkled all the brighter after the rains had washed through. I drifted out, too, and stood along the canal gazing down at the rippling water. My reflection shaped up on the surface, undulating in lozenges of color, and there was the cathedral floating behind me, its exterior a swirl of polychrome turrets and gilded onion domes.

In the US, after Kennedy was assassinated, the residents of Dallas bore a collective shame for what had happened in their midst, as if they had as a community pulled the trigger, not Lee Harvey Oswald. Dallas was dubbed the "City of Hate," and its contentious right-wing political climate was blamed for fomenting an assassination-poised environment.

By 2013, however, during fiftieth anniversary observances of the tragedy, Dallas found itself completely rehabilitated. Our country of course held no grudge whatsoever against the city or its people. News reports credited the popularity of the television show *Dallas* and also America's team, the Dallas Cowboys, for the successful rehab.

A tale of two cultures, there.

I smiled and watched a sightseeing boat skiff down the canal toward me, white caps ruffling as it passed. The Spilled Blood Cathedral disintegrated in the chop, its bell tower fluttering one way, its center dome wobbling another, its color drifting drifting, a kaleidoscope floating on the spray.

For Russia, на крови was the only path to redemption.

Football and TV were the American way.

★ ★ ★

Sources Cited

Wortman, Richard. "The Russian Style in Church Architecture." In *Architectures of Russian Identity, 1550 to the Present,* edited by Crackart, James and Rowland, Daniel. Ithaca, NY: Cornell University Press, 2003.

Andy Biggs

Andy Biggs
A Photographic Exhibit

ANDY BIGGS IS AN AVID ADVENTURER, conservationist, teacher, and outdoor photographer whose photography celebrates the African landscape and its rich wildlife, people, and culture. With a deep respect and understanding for African wildlife, Andy unfolds the world of the Serengeti, the Okavango Delta and other wildlife-rich destinations onto our doorstep with striking emotional depth. His photographic safaris allow the explorers to not only enhance their understanding of photography, lighting, and wildlife, but to develop a life-long admiration for Africa's beauty and culture.

In 2008, Banana Republic used thirteen of Andy's photographs as the cornerstone of their Urban Safari campaign, and his images were seen in all 750 stores around the globe, as well as on their billboards, catalogs and annual report. Andy was also the winner of the BBC Wildlife Photographer of the Year competition, Wild Places category, as well as a Highly Commended in the Unique Visions of Nature category.

★ ★ ★

★ ★ ★

Featured Art
from Andy Biggs
★   ★   ★

Lion Siblings

THREE LIONESSES WALKING

PENGUIN ON PACK ICE

SOLITUDE

ANTARCTICA III

SOUTH GEORGIA III

SOUTH GEORGIA IV

ICEBERG AND CLOUDED SUN

ICEBREAKER

FIGHTING HIPPOS

CHIMPANZEE XI

66

MOUNTAIN GORILLA VII

CHIMPANZEE I

CHIMPANZEE III

DEADVLEI I

FOUR ELEPHANTS IN A ROW

71

FLAMINGO TAKEOFF

STRETCHING LEOPARD

SPARRING WILDEBEEST

BLURRED RUNNING ZEBRAS

ELEPHANTS OVER THE OKAVANGO DELTA

ZEBRAS IN A ROW

GIRAFFE AND BABY

Terri Brown-Davidson

The Stieglitz Series on O'Keeffe

I THOUGHT: PERCEPTION'S A TRICKY THING. I stared at the stark white wall. A blue-black flower. No—a blood-bruise. Purple vulva? I touched my eyelids then blotted, with one of his oversized hankies, the sweat pooling beneath my breasts.

The house was quiet. Crickets outside, whirring black wings, though it was late, one a.m., two, an hour when my mother always said decent people would be in bed. The first time Stieglitz and I showed up at a midnight party, our arms twined around each other's waist, twins in black, matching capes flowing down to our boot tops, everybody laughed. And—for a second—I was mortified. Then, my spirit detached from the cocktails and crisp, linened tables, ascended to the ceiling, an O'Keeffe figure afloat in some hazy blue firmament.

I was floating, and I was free.

Then less free, suddenly: a housewife scrubbing a toilet bowl.

Through the filmy kitchen curtains, a glimpse of silvered moon. I leaned naked over the sink, eating my sandwich, letting the crumbs scatter across the porcelain sides, breasts resting sweaty atop my arms. A field stretched from the house out to the road, shadowy and black—not green—despite the moon. Stieglitz was asleep, thank God— even my calf muscles ached.

He'd posed me atop the bed. Stripped all the blankets off the mattress, made me fling myself into the air like a toddler. Not dignified, hell—not even attractive. Thinking about this, I picked at my sandwich, which had salami and onions in it, pepperoni, a generous heaping of lettuce. I knew that I'd reek tomorrow. Was glad.

Stieglitz would say that's because I'm a woman of many moods.

Perception's a tricky thing, yes. If you looked at me, maybe you'd think you saw an ordinary woman, brown hair going-to-gray coiled atop her head, eating her sandwich in quiet little bites then walking naked across her kitchen to nowhere, an empty coffee pot in her hand that she always forgot to fill with water. A dreamer, the most useless sort, gaunt, slack-breasted, thinking more about the dirty sheets she'd wadded up in the hamper yesterday than about her painting.

Or maybe you'd think you glimpsed, beneath the starved pallor of my flesh, the contours of the body Stieglitz already had immortalized in a hundred sepia-toned shots. Those thighs, you might murmur, those breasts—what myth, what magic— larger than life!

To which I'd reply, Thank you once again for all of your fucking bullshit.

I finished my sandwich, dropped the crumbs and wadded-up napkin in the sink. Wiped my mouth with the back of my hand before I shrugged on a nightgown I'd tossed to the kitchen floor, pulled on underwear, climbed the stairs to bed.

I WOKE WRAPPED IN SHEETS, glimpsed the glow in the hall from downstairs. Wasn't even certain I'd slept. We'd quarreled yesterday—the photographic series again.

"Alfred?" I called, massaging my back, sitting up against the headboard. "What the hell time is it, anyway."

He courted these early-morning sessions like a man might his whore. But it was the way we lived. It made no sense to other people, used to make sense to us, though the Bohemian lifestyle was tempting me less strongly these days. Peeling back the covers, I let the cold from the floorboards seep inside my nightgown, penetrate my underwear, the shock startling me conscious, making me clamp my legs closed though later, naked,

posing on a tabletop, straddling a folding chair, I'd become bored then simply numb.

I touched the wall. A smell of paraffin— he was burning candles again, proclaiming the day a celebration, each dawn a new opportunity for his pantheistic gods to bestow their bounty.

And me?

When he wasn't so scary-eyed intense that he frightened the bejesus out of me, he was the most ridiculous man I'd ever met.

So I descended the stairs to a blaze so assaultive it's a wonder the patched walls of our house didn't snatch up every flame, create a full-fledged conflagration.

Exhaustion shrouded me so tightly my limbs seemed squeezed against my torso. I waited for dry-eyed, benevolent strangers to lower me into the ground.

HE WAS SITTING AT THE ROUND little table where we shared our morning coffee, regarding me with a smile just slightly salacious. A rakish man though ancient, dear God, a shock of white hair rising electrified from the crown of his pinkish head, his skinny arms protruding from the folds of a black woolen cape, even at this hour. A vigorous man, yet broken-down, and much, much older than me.

I'd been a fool to pursue him. Not to mention the fact that he'd deserted his wife for me. And daughter. Which made me, I suppose—irrespective of the photos—a dyed-in-the-wool wanton.

"Georgie," he said, and his dry lips curled ever so imperceptibly. "Or should I say 'Lady Lazarus.'"

"I got two hours of sleep. Look at me—I'm a mess! How do you expect me to function?"

He leaned forward, eyeing me. Cupped his massive hand under my chin, tilted my face back to inspect it more clearly in the rampant candle-glow. I could well imagine the bright orange flames chasing shadows across my cheekbones, the oily pools of darkness beneath my eyes. He wasn't being sadistic. I'd fallen into his muse-category this morning: Georgia the woman, Georgia the painter, would, this day, no longer exist.

"I can work with it," he said.

"*It.*"

So," ALFRED WAS SAYING, "I thought I'd experiment more with lighting today. Bring out those shadows under your eyes. Highlight them."

He lifted the big silver coffee pot, poured my brew black and steaming into the ceramic white mug I favored. I loved the sensation of drug-strong caffeine blasting my veins.

"You mean," I said, "make me look like a monster."

Alfred shrugged. "It's all about drama, isn't it?"

"I'd say it's about identity." I stood up then, my nightie rumpling across my breasts, which were beginning to feel, under Alfred's attention, pendulous.

"Where are you going?" Alfred demanded.

"I'm starving. So hungry I could eat a cow. It's Sunday, in case you hadn't noticed. The proverbial day of rest."

"We're not religious folks."

"How about privacy? Is there ever a necessity for that?"

Regarding me, Alfred replied, "I can never get enough of your company. We're a family now, Georgie. You know what that implies."

"Suffocation," I snapped. I walked to the coat rack in the foyer, struggled into my black wool cape, my nightgown peeking out. Stooping, I pulled on then laced up my boots.

"Where the hell are you going?" This time, it was Alfred staring at his coffee cup, refusing to meet my eyes.

"I'm going to go find a cow. Kill it with my strong bare hands. Eat it bloodied, raw. And when I'm done, I'm going for a nice long walk. Clear the fog out of my head."

"It's three o'clock in the morning," Alfred replied. "We're out in the middle of nowhere. You might be hurt. Killed."

I opened the front door, stepped out into the dark.

ALFRED DIDN'T KNOW ABOUT THE CAFÉ only a half mile out of town. I'd stumbled upon it, had no intention of revealing my discovery. Because—and I still believe this—there are places within the soul, spaces so private that to allow others to enter is to risk tearing holes in the inner landscapes we all inhabit, both the most solitary and luminous terrain we possess.

And that's what I felt like, a plethora of holes, as if any stranger might be able to peer through my pockings.

I stepped out into a blackness phosphorescent with moonlight, my high-laced boots navigating the steps. I didn't turn back once to glance at the house, a disaster we were renting from a nearby farmer in Wessley, a small town in upstate New York, for just enough money to justify his not having it razed.

How I despised that house, its peeling paint, dappled flecks of off-white crumbling off the walls, a basement so dank and spider infested it crawled up two stories every night to inject my dreams with a shot of pure horror.

I descended the steps as a cat somewhere yowled, allowed my boots to carry me to the dirt road that few cars traveled though I always glanced at them admiringly—I adored a black-painted Model A, dreamed of owning one someday myself, climbing up on the running board with a fat roll of paintings under my arm and then settling into the seat before I let the steering wheel whirl left, right, left, guiding me to parts unknown, the mystery enticing me, old Alfred left behind ephemeral as a dust bunny.

I walked faster along the road, my cape wind-blasted, shadowy leaves floating around my face.

I loved being by myself. Loved how the moonlight covered me. Why was it that everything seemed perfect when I was alone, damaged when I encountered others?

Within ten minutes I was there. A hand-scrawled sign, "Sam's Roadside Café," the letters eroded after years of mud and rain. If Sam Donahue had been in business for the money, he wouldn't have allowed his café to stay open in a second double-shift from midnight to six a.m., when few customers—work-dazed, drunk—came crawling in to dangle like lead-footed flies from the walls.

But Sam was a wealthy landowner who craved the company of loners and artisans, adoring me, honestly, because I was an Artist Who'd Almost Made It.

And of course Sam knew about Alfred, Wessley being the most miniscule of towns. The great Alfred Stieglitz! My mentor, captor, Svengali. Word had leaked out about Alfred's latest project—photographs of my body—though Alfred wasn't willing to discuss the details with anybody, either hicks or sophisticates.

I went inside. The café walls were always a shock, the throbbing, rich red of arterial blood, a shade Sam associated with artistry. The booths, fortunately, were a muted shade of taupe, homey and comfy, taped together to help them retain their stuffing. I headed straight to the booth nearest the jukebox, "Georgie's Spot."

There were three other customers that night. Mel J. Pakula, a local craftsman who hawked Fabergé-egg knockoffs, slumped beneath his comb-over, nursing a root beer in a mug. Melanie Gatskon, the New York City renegade who we all suspected turned tricks on the side, was eating mashed potatoes, her lips redder than the walls, her black-stockinged legs angling sideways out of the booth, gray-wool skirt tugged down over her knees. She might've been a hooker, but she refused to remain a stereotype. I respected her for that.

But the last customer compelled me the most—my best female friend, Susan Atkinson.

Susan was everything I wasn't, and how could that not intrigue me? A sumptuous redhead whose plush hair draped her buttocks, a woman built long and lean as a giraffe, she was at once odd, irresistible, and talented. Eyeing Susan, I had to restrain myself from winking. She spotted me just as fast, rose adjusting her kimono-style dress (an emerald so bright it blinded me), sat down across from me in the booth.

A whistle, long and low. I can tell you it emerged from *moi*. "Putting on the dog," I said. "A little atypical for Wessley, wouldn't you say?"

"Well," Susan said, "at least I'm not still in my nightgown."

My face got hot.

She plucked a tattered menu from the table rack, pretended to scan it though she'd memorized every item. "Also," Susan said, "just because I live in a cow town doesn't mean I have to dress like the heifers."

I relaxed. "Now you're talking. Let's blow this joint, baby. Head on down to New Mexico. The colors are so brilliant there I've heard they induce strokes."

"That's you, Georgie. Not me."

"Make it you," I said, but hated my pleading tone.

"Georgie," she said, her voice measured and low, and then the waiter—Sam's only flunky, a greasy boy with pimples, string tie knotted noose-like around his throat—wandered over with a pot. "You hungry?" he asked, and I nodded.

"Ravenous."

My finger stabbing menu items, I ordered a fat glazed doughnut, hash browns, a glass of tomato juice, and an extra hot cup of coffee with plenty of cream on top. Pimple Boy shook his head as he walked away, wiping his hands on his apron, tucking his pencil behind his ear.

"Jesus," Susan said, after he'd vanished. "What's going on with you? You're too skinny to handle all that food."

"Can't gain any weight," I said. "Just keep losing and losing."

"Georgie—he's not still working on this project?"

"Day and night," I said, and laughed. "Night and pre-fucking-dawn."

"This isn't healthy. You've got to get out of here. Is he ever taking you back to 291? Is he ever going to exhibit you again?"

"This is his time," I said, looking at Susan's beautifully proportioned form. I refused to envy her, even when she landed a show, even when she told me, later, she was going back to New York City, had only moved to Wessley in the first place to keep me company.

I listened carefully, nodded at the appropriate intervals, launched into my food with gusto when Pimple Boy brought it, food seeming—at that time—my most definite connection to the world. And Susan talked for what seemed hours, my neck stiff from nodding. I was used to people, both men and women, falling in love with me all the time, and, though nice, it exhausted me.

But when Susan suggested Leaf Skinny-Dipping, a visit to her studio in the woods, I woke up.

"Yes?" she asked, reaching across the table, grabbing my hand.

"Yes," I said, and closed my eyes, the dark calming me.

"Goodbye, Sam's Café," I whispered, dropping a tip on the table, as Susan went to the counter and paid Pimple Boy for our meal.

Goodbye, Red Walls, as if I'd never glimpse them again, though I believed then that I'd die and be buried in Wessley.

WE TRAMPED FOR MINUTES through the woods before locating the spot: Leaf Skinny-Dipping, a game Susan introduced me to when she'd visited me at Lake George, was best undertaken with layers of leaf cover to cushion the impact of the ground against frailer joints and bones. I loved to play, loved the woods where I was certain nobody would find me, adored Susan's studio-cabin, which contained all of the mystery Alfred's and my rental house lacked, none of the dilapidation.

As Susan walked, a near-comical sight in high heels, her ankles bowing toward each other, moonlight flashed like fish scales on her dress, shining greener here, blacker, as if we'd plunged into an ocean world of trees, shadows, dead and dried-out leaves.

Susan heard me laugh, but who the hell could help it? It was as if the Lady of Shalott had abandoned her tower.

"Fuck you," she snapped, without turning around, when I kept laughing.

When she tugged off her right high-heel, hopping like a one-legged crane, I knew we were nearing the Site of Moonlit Bliss. I

bent, grabbed at my boot laces: Susan was faster, kicked the other shoe off, strode on.

I managed to shed one boot before I stood up and hurried after.

We emerged into the clearing Susan had selected, the trees forming a stark-branched, near claustrophobic circle of privacy.

Susan paused then, facing me, before she undid the snaps on her kimono, snap-snapping them all the way down as if she were a soldier casting off her brilliantly decorated military jacket, slipping out of her skirt, something formal even about her disrobing, and in seconds she was standing in front of me in her bra, stockings, panties, garters, everything black, everything sensual, a sexiness I could never aspire to.

"Now you," she teased; I shook my head.

"What's the problem? Not worried about Old Man Alfred? Who—good God, Georgie—has hair in his nose?"

"I'm wearing his shorts."

"What?"

"I'm wearing his boxers. And—there are holes."

She stared. "Christ, Georgie. You used to be a sexy woman. Those little girl dresses! Men's-cut suits! What's happening?"

"I don't know," I said, glancing down, "but I've got to resist it, don't I?"

So, while she watched me, I undressed, pulled off my nightgown, shucked off the offending boxers so quickly I was scarcely conscious of my liberation. But that was my goal, now, to make everything conscious, psychically available so I could rub it like a stone between my hands, memorize every facet.

I stood naked in front of Susan, shivering and skinny. Still, bless her, she didn't criticize me, and in seconds we'd approached the mound Susan must have shoveled earlier into the center of the clearing.

It was an incredible assemblage. This time, I was convinced, Susan had achieved perfection. It was—hell—nearly aesthetic. Though it was dark and I couldn't physically see every leaf, my painter's mind brought all their colors to life. A perfect mixture of red, gold, mauve, yellow, purple, brown, gray, off-ivory. Not many of the colors touched each other, yet the swirl of varying hues lured the eye down and down and down into a leaf maelstrom. They were too gorgeous to violate, yet I plucked a large red maple leaf off the pile, my sudden saliva rush startling me because I knew what it boded. Fuck, I wanted to paint. I tugged at a yellow leaf, shining with moonlight that poured straight down over the clearing and stroked everything below it with a luscious burnished glow. "Shh," Susan whispered, removing the leaves from my hand, careful not to tear or crumple them, "it isn't time for that yet." She replaced the leaves as if she were Mr. Pakula handling his own fake Fabergé egg.

"Ready?" Susan asked, her eyes cutting away from me, her gaze lifting toward the tops of the naked branches, the utterly black sky lit with yellow moon. She's memorizing this spot, wants to remember it forever, I thought, and then we were both falling forward, tumbling naked into the scattering mound of fabulously roughened textures, snapped or damaged leaves, the frail debris crushed beneath our bodies, red, yellow, and the occasional green thrusting up around us until those leaves pushed up over our chests and necks, buried all traces of our bodies, and then we were lying on our backs, sprawling there as spent and breathless as if we'd come.

I ENTERED SUSAN'S CABIN as if it were a sanctuary. Slow-burning balsam-fir candles set upright on plates, books tossed about on two gold couches—*The Spiritual in Art*, Zen Buddhism, Japanese line drawings—battered coffee tables placed before each couch where we often lounged, drinking jasmine tea.

There was a bathroom not large enough for a Pekingese to turn around in, a detached sink with tarnished faucets, a toilet that routinely required the assistance of the plunger Susan had left wedged against the bowl.

A kitchen Susan never cooked in, visible from the entryway.

But—of course—there was also that marvelous room behind the living room, dedicated entirely to Susan's painting.

The daughter of a socialite, Susan had the means, when she bought this cabin, to have the Painting Room built to specification, the result an immense, uncluttered space with an adjustable skylight that could let in degrees of natural light or—if the day was cloudy—be closed to switch to an artificial system that gave her more than adequate painting light.

Several canvases in progress always occupied this room, and, whenever I left, I dreamed of constructing rooms so light-saturated that sometimes they lacked even ceilings, houses whose roofs I might access

85

with a tall, tall ladder that plunged me into the center of a white-burning circle of stars.

"Tea?" Susan asked, picking leaves out her hair. "Or I have a little coffee left over from this morning." From a closet she brought out two robes that we put on. I stooped and folded Susan's clothes and my nightwear she'd tossed on the floor. I paused a second to align our boots, too, which she'd also flung aside.

"Coffee, thanks," I said. She went to the kitchen, poured.

"Susan? Why won't you show me your new paintings?"

She handed me my coffee. I sipped it, touched my mouth. "Too old," I said.

She put her cup on the coffee table. Examined her hands, then glanced at a print of Van Gogh's "Wheatfield with Crows" that she'd thumb-tacked to the wall. "Not sure that's such a good idea."

"Because you think I have nothing going on."

"Because I think you haven't encountered yourself yet."

I followed her to the couch; we sat down together, pulling away when our thighs brushed. "Now—what the hell does that mean?"

She hesitated, picked at a cuticle. From this angle, I couldn't see her eyes. "Just that there's nothing about yourself that you acknowledge," she said. "My love for you. Your sexuality. What this whole photographic series is doing to you. Jesus, to your painting."

"Maybe I was wrong," I said. "Maybe the world doesn't care about my painting."

Susan looked back at me.

"What?" She was staring.

"Susan," I said finally, "stop it, OK? A ghost's walking across my grave."

Susan smiled then, watching me. "I don't understand you," she said. "You have everything, Georgie. You're free."

"Don't see how. There's nobody more encumbered."

Susan studied her thumbnail. "I envy you," she said. "The parties, recognition."

"Bullshit. You're more lauded than I am, and you know it."

"But you're like a woman without a past, waiting to be seduced. When you could do anything you wanted."

"I have no idea where you're headed with this discussion."

She paused. Then, rising, she laughed, went to an oak curio cabinet in the corner, opened the glass door, took out a gilt-edged porcelain bird, very fine. Returning, she handed it to me, but I refused to take it— she knew I was scared of breakage. "Do you know where I got this?" Susan asked.

"Japan?"

"I remember nothing about the trip. But I do remember every shop." She smiled.

"You're not shallow," I said. "You're an artist."

She sat down across from me, cradling the bird in the folds of her robe. "Georgie," she said. "Do you know what happens when a woman has a baby?"

"What're you talking about?"

"When a woman who's a painter has a baby."

I looked away. I didn't want to know.

"Something happens," Susan said. "OK?"

And drew a breath, one finger tracing the bird's tiny beak. "Something happens after a woman gives birth, not with the woman herself, you understand, but with the world—it's as if there's this massive, tacitly agreed-upon realignment of expectations."

I kept looking away.

"Maybe you don't get it," Susan said, stroking a wing. "Or—I don't know—can't. But it's like a shift in the surface of the Earth. Plate Tectonics 101. Do you understand what I'm saying? The woman goes into the experience thinking, OK, I'll give birth to this child. And I'll love her, and I'll take care of her, and she'll be part of my contribution to the world.

"But the world disagrees with her, Georgie. All at once, the world doesn't want her contributions anymore. The needs of the child are endless, repetitive. And the woman—the woman—begins to feel her self siphoned away.

"At first it's so slow it's imperceptible. She gets out of bed in the morning, thinking not, oh, I forgot to wash out my brushes last night, but, instead, oh, I don't have a stack of clean clothes for the baby.

"And gradually she becomes aware that her mind is crammed with such thoughts. And that her self is located somewhere in the part of her brain that seems to be dying because of a host of pragmatic concerns she'd never anticipated, which the world now insists she fulfill.

"Never let the child even whimper from hunger; therefore, keep the breast available. Or the child has a nosebleed. A caca on the sheets. Strip the crib—hand-wash the linen—scalding water—read it a book—read it a dozen—sing two thousand songs to stimulate its little brain."

"Susan," I said, and grabbed her hand, kissed it; some coffee spilled on the carpet. She pushed me away then pushed the bird into my palm, folding my fingers over it.

"Fuck it, Georgie! You know I'm right." Her face was getting red, and I wanted to hug her, wanted to cry, but did nothing except hold the bird in one hand and my coffee cup in the other. "Clawing hands," Susan continued, and touched my wrist. "Shitty diapers, the baby chewing her nipple. Like in that Goya painting?—'Saturn Devouring His Son'—she becomes that tiny, near-invisible figure in white, squeezed to death in the claws of the monster before her head's snapped off in one bloody attack.

"But, fuck it, she's still alive—she starts to fight back. Starts getting up at two in the morning to paint. Tends the baby by day, keeps the house mopped, dustless, spotless because the fucking husband and his parents insist on it.

"But the baby's not to be outwitted. It senses the woman's secret life, and it wants that too, because that's the nature of children—they're ravenous.

"Soon the woman's exhausted. Can't even articulate the thought—because it's so fucking painful, right? But the husband's happy. And the baby's delighted, because, of course, it owns her now."

A little scrap of skin had come loose from Susan's cuticle. She pinched it between her left forefinger, thumb, while I stared, but she only sat there. Until I asked,

"Who has it now?"

Susan paused, dropped the scrap. "Minnesota," she said. "With my parents. I think—she's going on five."

"*Think*," I said, but wasn't accusing her. "God." I leaned over, hugged her, her body going stiff. "I still want to see your paintings," I said, rubbing her back; she stayed rigid.

"I don't know," Susan said. "Maybe next time.

"Hell, it's six in the morning! The sun's coming up. Everyday I have to watch. It's like a physical necessity with me, you know? We could grab a beer, go outside, lie down on the grass. Or what's left of it, because it's dead. You don't mind a few bugs?"

"I'd better be getting home to Alfred," I said. "He'll be wondering where I've gone."

"To change his diapers?" Susan asked.

And—just as she'd expected—neither of us smiled.

I PULLED MY SHORTS ON, nightgown, cape, tugged on my boots then crouched to lace them up. Walked home, pinkish light illuminating my big-knuckled hands, my boots dragging through leaf cover, my body beneath the black wrap still thrumming from my memory of the game.

If Georgia, alone in the forest, has an orgasm that nobody witnesses, has she actually experienced it?

I supposed it depended on how much I trusted my own reality.

T HE DAWN SKY FLOODED OUR HOUSE the spectral hue of mourning in some countries, China, for instance, stark white, not bone, the color of bones much less savory than anybody would admit, a murky yellow unlike the whiteness associated with skeletons.

The color of the house filthy, yet strangely compelling.

A little like Alfred himself.

How had it started? I'd worked on some new drawings, different drawings, abstractions, not like the silly dead rabbit and copper pot I'd won a prize for at school. I liked them; they seemed real. Who should I give them to? Spreading them out on the floor, touching the drawings just lightly with my fingertips to not smear the charcoal, I let my hands decide as I addressed the mailing tube in which I'd rolled up and rubber banded them.

And then, it became more complicated.

I gave them to my dear friend Anita, who gave them to the great Stieglitz.

Stieglitz, who was boomingly gregarious, who was always surrounded by his artists at 291.

Who always fell in love with the newest and most talented sycophant.

Not that I didn't like the other followers—especially Paul Strand, who was, physically, so much more beautiful than the beaten-down Alfred—but I couldn't bear hordes of people. I wanted to live alone and now here I was with Alfred, who jabbered about nothing until I ran into the back room to hide, curling tiny in a corner. Surrounded yet isolated in a place where the terrain was rugged but not lovely, I craved desert, cactus, sand. The reds, purples, sadistically violent gold of late-autumn leaves, black flowers unfurling lush petals. I yearned for them and woke many nights, my mouth flooded with color.

But even my painting had deserted me, though I remained obsessed with my palette, as a woman who's been a prima ballerina recalls her soiled toe shoes, the hammer she used to relax the succulent silk.

A poor analogy.

I lived inside those colors.

Those colors kept me alive.

Alfred photographing me in simple black and white.

I bedraggled myself into the house, and he was there, his shaggy white head tucked under his black camera-cloth. "Georgie," he said, pulling out. "You OK? You left hours ago."

"I can't live like this anymore." This wasn't what I meant to say, despising bad taste even in sentiment.

"What're you talking about?"

"You said you'd stop at a hundred," I said. "One hundred fucking photographs. And you're really just getting warmed up! When will it stop? When will you stop chasing me? I want my painting back, Alfred. I want my painting back now."

Alfred paused. Then he moved away from the camera, moved around it. I studied him. He was old, so old. How much time did he have? Some people described him as vigorous, but I saw the truth. Some people described him as a philanderer, but he'd made me his muse. And how much was that worth? I knew the value of the photographs. I knew that he was recreating me in a way no woman on Earth had ever had the opportunity to be recreated. I wasn't, through his renderings, sack-breasted, thin-hipped Georgia but iconic, my hands elegant, my chignon sleek under the hats he set back on my head, my plain face carved from shadows, luminous when the light slanted across it and bathed my eyes brighter than stars swarming like honeybees over our house.

A woman on paper, *his* paper.

Still, it was a gift.

"Georgie," Alfred said. "This project is my baby."

I remembered what Susan had said, glanced at my hands, couldn't quite see them, everything far away, farther away than I wanted it to be.

"Well, all right then. I've got to respect that. Where do you want me this morning?"

"Living room. On top of the radiator. It's a difficult pose. Legs up, toes curled under: we'll have to take a lot of breaks."

"So you can see my——."

He didn't like the word. Though he never would've admitted it, especially after he himself had brought the Rodin drawings of female genitalia into 291, those exquisite sworls of hair, delicate, pinkish clitorises, precisely rendered.

"Yes," Alfred said, fussing with his camera in the foyer, where he'd been set up, hoping, I knew, that I'd come home. Without me, I knew as well, he'd still be shooting the street scenes and clouds he essayed when his muse wasn't present, for Alfred confused inspiration and love.

So I gave him time.

Allowed him to shift his camera, collapse the tripod, reassemble the whole black mechanical mess in the living room. And, when he was ready, I followed him there, shedding clothes as I walked. My breasts, released, swung forward against my breastbone, my shoulders rounded, the cold air of this drafty house drifting up between my thighs. I was conscious—hyperconscious, really—of the yellow quality my skin acquired in certain lights. But I was a good sport. I pushed myself up on the radiator, squatted there with my legs angled open, my toes gripping the metallic grill, my hands reaching back for balance when I had difficulty maintaining the pose, little flickers of fire licking the backs of my calves.

"Higher," Alfred said. "Push yourself higher. Open up more."

AND THAT'S WHAT I DID, though my mind was pulling me back, back to the paintings Susan hadn't allowed me to look at because she believed my own creativity would be paralyzed by such a lavish assortment of beauties, the surreal green horses she loved to paint, their black-nosed nostrils distended in gusts of red-orange flame, the white sheep drifting heavenward with the lofting, comical rapture of the most buoyant clouds.

I tracked all of these images in my mind and then, I let them go. I shifted higher up, clenching the radiator with fingertips that burned to the bone, the camera lens regarding me like a black-and-white eye that recorded, as I did, the value of the aesthetic.

Bruce Bennett

A Further Message to Lucasta

"To Lucasta, Going to the Wars"
— Richard Lovelace

It's true I do love _Honour_ more,
    Or I would not depart.
I need a battle to restore
    And heal my wounded heart.

I need the clash of men at arms
    To give me peace and rest
And shield me from the potent charms
    Of your unyielding breast!

Call it inconstancy. It's you
    Who drive me to the field.
But I will stay here and be true
    If you decide to yield.

Yes, I will stay here and be true,
    Though all the world deplore
The sort of man who would choose you
    Instead of go to war!

John Christopher Nelson

Sola Fide

JACQUI GAUGHAN HAD A VALID—though, she felt, inexcusable—reason for being late to the prom. The unforeseen limousine fire didn't make her feel any better about missing everything that had happened prior to her arrival. Nor did the lateness of the others in her party make her own lateness any more bearable. Once she entered the gymnasium and spotted Howard Brandt and heard Madonna—the guy she'd been waiting all day to see and the song she'd been hoping all day to hear—everyone else in her group ceased to matter.

After dancing with Howard, Jacqui would find out:

1. "Footloose" was the second song to play—it was within the first three to play at last year's prom, homecoming, and winter formal. Jacqui wondered how many more formals would endure Kenny Loggins' onslaught;

2. Donny Styles pregamed too hard by himself in his stepmom's basement and was already passed out in the back of a pickup in the parking lot, ruining the tux he borrowed from his uncle Todd;

3. Tailor Rinks left the dance abruptly when her younger, prettier sister, Leslie—most people supposed they were only half-related—told Tailor she looked fat in her dress. Leslie had been drinking. Tailor had not.

But before she learned any of this, Jacqui's only concern was seeing Howard, catching his eye before he and his date left to fool around. Jacqui was sure that if Howard and Suzie Cramer hadn't already had sex, Suzie would put out tonight.

By the time Jacqui arrived, she was already upset about the electric-blue dress she was wearing. The dress did not look bad on her. She looked better than many of the girls in attendance, who had all seemingly embraced the current anti-coke trend and put on a ton of weight in the last year. Jacqui still did coke here and there. She used the word "recreational" and didn't feel it had anything to do with her not putting on weight. But for Jacqui it didn't matter that she looked better, it was that the other girls—not just at Valhalla, but at every other high school in San Diego, California, perhaps the nation—were wearing carnation-pink dresses tonight. That's what was hip this year, this season, this moment in 1985. So far tonight, Jacqui felt tragically unhip.

Three weeks later, reviewing the photos taken before the dance, Jacqui neglected to comment on her date and simply conceded to herself, "You look like Donna Lea. Christ." Earlier that year, Jacqui pierced her right ear a second and third time to mimic her friend Donna Lea and, in response to her efforts, earned no praise from her supposed friend but instead the scolds of her own father for being "less than trailer trash." Yes, for the piercings. Ear piercings.

But this feeling of tragic unhipness only lasted during the few moments between her arrival and when her song started to play. "Crazy For You" was already popular that year, but was nothing particularly special to anyone but Jacqui, who had already based her night's imagined success on whether or not the song would play.

Her date, Kenneth Kauffman, was not her first choice. Jacqui had recently left Bob Garber and her brothers had suggested Kenneth for a date. He was not ugly, but handsome was not a word anyone would use. He was too nice for her. Especially after Bob. Bob, who had already graduated. Bob, who sold drugs. Bob, who explained away rogue panties discovered in his apartment. Someone gentlemanly like Kenneth felt foreign, unpleasant.

Her older brothers were among the first two classes to graduate from Valhalla in 1976

and 1977. The school had been erected to endure the overflow from other El Cajon high schools, which were unable to accommodate the region's exploding population. Kenneth was in Jacqui's class and his older brother was a friend of her brothers. Jacqui and Kenneth would share the Valhalla class of 1985 stamp on their diplomas, but little else besides that.

★ ★ ★

MARY AND MARIA PERNICANO AND DONNA LEA and their dates went to dinner at Tom Ham's Lighthouse. Kenneth and his friends Marcus Szinski and Bud Lauftner had chosen something more modest for Jacqui, Tammy Strellic, and Amy Anderson: Fletcher Bowl.

The menu was not quite as extensive as the one Tom Ham offered. Fletcher Bowl had the standard bowling alley fare of hotdogs, hamburgers, fries, and pitchers of beer, the last of which the kids weren't old enough to order. But this wouldn't interfere with Jacqui's thigh-bound flask of Southern Comfort—which she wouldn't ever be able to stomach again after the summer of 1988. As for the flask, it was not comfortable, nor was it the least bit subtle. But Jacqui felt it was cool, mature. She imagined Howard would appreciate it, if he were to touch her leg and discover the flask. He would smile at her knowingly, maybe even wink.

Walking into Fletcher Bowl made the imminent disappointment of their dinner more tolerable. Just after the initial six notes of "Everybody Wants to Rule the World," the teens pushed through the doors and made their way toward the café in the back corner of the bowling alley, the song's guitar riff leading their way from the stereo speakers hanging off the walls above the casino-style carpet.

As for Jacqui's date, Kenneth would eventually become handsome enough. Nobody remarkable, but decent, better than Jacqui would give him credit for. He would end up marrying someone more attractive than him—more attractive than Jacqui. For now, that didn't matter. They were at a bowling alley. And Jacqui was about to eat a plain cheeseburger ("I'm fine without fries,") while Donna Lea was probably feasting on swordfish or piling in paella. In fact, Donna Lea was enjoying bouillabaisse, which Jacqui had never heard of and would never see on a menu.

Back to Kenneth. Sometimes youth is easier for everyone if braces are imagined as invisible. Weighing braces too heavily in high school dating decisions rules out many otherwise qualified candidates. But they are just so unavoidable. As Jacqui's tongue and teeth took in the vast array of texture and flavor offered by the complexities of Fletcher Bowl's head chef Ricky Chavez's burger, she watched Kenneth eating his. He was not careful to keep his lips closed and, even within her passing glances, Jacqui could see burger debris clotted into the wedges of the metal wires surrounding his teeth. Also, he had small hands. He was not shorter than her but not taller either, with eyes dark enough to be mysterious to high school girls but not dark enough to cause genuine intrigue. His hair had just enough of a curl to suggest a Jewish mother or

father—maybe both—but Jacqui didn't care that much.

Just as Jacqui was imagining sitting across from Howard, some place nicer than this, Kenneth leaned in too close, bringing a series of chin blemishes into view. "Are you excited to dance later?"

Jacqui nodded a curt, impassive, "Yes," before slipping off to the bathroom.

She stood in the mirror and judged her dress again. Jacqui frowned at her hips as she pulled the dress down. It was too early in the night for it to be riding up. But the dress was too tight and her hips were too big. And her too-small breasts looked even smaller, pulled taut against her chest. Jacqui set the flask she'd removed from her garter on the counter and scooped her hand into the corset top to pull her breasts up into the spotlight. Jacqui was certain the sex she'd had with Bob would not be beat by Kenneth, not even met. Still, she was feeling gamesome, even if unsure whether she would allow Kenneth to kiss her.

Semi-satisfied with her reflection, despite her dress color, Jacqui pulled another swallow from her flask. There were still three shot-sized bottles nestled in the bottom of her purse. She emptied one into the flask, before throwing the bottle away. She planned to top off the flask again before entering the dance.

★ ★ ★

YEARS LATER, IN 1992, this was the part of the night that stood out most. There wasn't anything all that remarkable about the moment, but sitting in her hospital bed, Jacqui would catch a flash of herself behind her eyelids. Electric-blue dress, messed beach hairdo, and a chrome flask, all of them reflecting bathroom mirror light. The memory, the image, was colored by a haze not of nostalgia, but as if the memory had been recorded with eighties-quality cameras and film.

At twenty-five Jacqui would be diagnosed with undifferentiated, high-grade sarcoma, an extremely rare form of cancer that manifested as a large grapefruit, or small-sized melon, depending on who told the story, on the outside of the thigh on which she'd worn her flask seven years earlier.

The cancer was as aggressive as it was rare. The treatment was equally aggressive and Jacqui lost all of her hair and dropped from one hundred and nineteen pounds to ninety-seven. Her doctors were certain she would die and told her as politely as they could manage that she might consider saying good-byes, resolving conflicts, maybe checking some things off her list. Jacqui stared at the hospital wall. She had no idea what to do first. She had already performed her life's most brazen act seven years earlier.

Her mother was also in the room and chose to ignore the doctors, deciding her parental intuition outweighed their education and practice. And, by a complete fluke, her mother was right. Jacqui survived.

Back in 1985, this did nothing for Jacqui. No, tonight, prom night, Jacqui would return from the bathroom, having rinsed her mouth in the sink and relipsticked, adjusted her breasts one last time, to see that everyone else was finished eating and the bill was paid—she guessed Kenneth had paid for her, but did not thank him.

Although the group had arrived at the bowling alley in Kenneth's parents' van, the big surprise of the night was waiting outside. The limo was nothing impressive. Tuxedo black-and-white, short enough to be mistaken for a hearse, but providing the advantage of looking larger in the context of a bowling alley parking lot. It would fit all of them, and it was a limo. The gesture was kind, so Jacqui, Amy, and Tammy all did their best, without conferring, to feign excitement and surprise in equal volume. This, of course, after standing around awkwardly while Kenneth passed the van keys off to his mother, who had shown up in her nightgown with a flannel over her shoulders, to collect them.

In the limo, Tammy declared, "I hope they play REO Speedwagon."

Amy rolled her eyes. "No way."

"Way. It's romantic."

"Excuse me?"

"It's romantic."

"REO Speedwagon?"

"Yeah. What?"

"Jacqui, back me up on this," Amy pleaded.

Kenneth, Marcus, and Bud were staring out their windows, pretending not to listen to the debate.

"They're fine," Jacqui answered, not wanting to take sides. "Anyway, there's just one song I want to hear tonight," and it was much more romantic than anything REO Speedwagon had or would ever release. Their music was the kind jocks got laid to, and it would never be romantic.

"What song?"

Jacqui was deciding whether or not to share the answer when the limo shrugged into an abrupt halt, causing her to spill from the flask she was sipping from between conversational cues. Before she could say anything, the driver was pulling open the back door and yelling at everyone, "Get out! Now!"

Upon exiting the vehicle, initially unsure if they were being robbed or kidnapped, the group froze and observed the flames shooting from the cracks between the hood and the body of the limo. While everyone else continued to stare, Jacqui's eyes wandered to the limo driver with the car phone in his hand, the cord stretched to its full extent. She assumed a manager or dispatcher or something on the other end of the line, maybe the fire department. She turned and walked to the gas station across the street. At the pay phone, she called a cab.

"Actually," she added, turning around to see the limo now fully enveloped in flames and everyone else, including the driver, watching it with their arms akimbo, "can I make it two cabs?"

The boys weren't allowed a vote in Jacqui's decision to split the group, the girls in one cab, the boys in the other.

In their cab, Amy asked the other two, "So?"

"I feel like," Tammy started, looking at Jacqui to verify, "Kenneth isn't getting any tonight."

"He wasn't to begin with," Jacqui answered, adding another bottle of SoCo to the flask, her corsage and the dark obscuring her action from their cabdriver.

The girls had taken the first of the two cabs and made it to the dance before the boys. Tammy wanted to wait for them out front, but Jacqui said, "They'll find us," without meaning it or caring, and headed toward the entrance of the dance. Amy followed.

Upon entering, Jacqui scanned the crowd, observed the ocean of carnation-pink—held her judgment till later when she was alone in her bed—and spotted Howard and his date. Just as her song started to play.

She knew it from the first beats of the drum. She put a hand firmly against Amy's arm to suggest she not follow, and strode across the room toward Howard, who was making small talk with his date. Just before the first lyrics of the song, Jacqui had her hand on Howard's, her eyes on Suzie's glance of reproach.

"Would you mind if I stole a quick dance?"

Suzie's barely hidden scowl, her too-heavily caked makeup, the volume of hairspray in her hair all suggested that yes, she would mind. But Suzie managed a, "No," and a disingenuous follow-up smile. Howard noticed none of this. His eyes were on Jacqui's, half-confused, half-interested, escorted onto the dance floor as Madonna sang, "I see you through the smoky air, can't you feel the weight of my stare?"

The two had just started to sway together—one set of hands clasped, the other two on shoulder and hip, respectively, pelvises much closer than polite for two people who had shared barely a "Hello" before this moment—when Madonna explained, "What I'm dying to say . . ."

Jacqui and Howard maintained eye contact for the duration of "Crazy For You."

Kenneth and the other two showed up halfway though the song. While Kenneth stood and watched, Marcus and Bud stole off with Tammy and Amy.

When the song ended, Howard started to say something, probably adolescent and unimportant, but Jacqui stopped him. She brought her face close to his ear, kissed its lobe, and whispered, "It's fine." Then she walked away, with all the satisfaction she had imagined and more.

That was her last interaction with Howard, who would marry Suzie, as Marcus would marry Tammy, and Bud would marry Amy. Jacqui was not often a topic in Howard and Suzie's home, but was a reason to spend an evening in silence each of the four times her name was mentioned during the twelve years of their marriage. Even into their twenties and thirties, Howard and Suzie's two daughters would occasionally wonder out loud to each other, "Who was this Jacqui person? What could she possibly have done?"

Before Madonna and Jacqui and Howard were finished dancing, Kenneth had excused himself from the dance entirely. That was the last Jacqui ever heard from him as well, excluding details through the gossip train of friends.

In the hospital bed in 1992, when Jacqui remembered her image in the Fletcher Bowl bathroom mirror, the thought inevitably leading to the rest of the night, a too-small part of her wanted to feel bad for Kenneth. But she didn't. She knew he was fine. He lived. Everyone lives, despite their fleeting, superficial pains.

And, most important to her, Jacqui would also live.

Photo by John Haney

AMANDA JERNIGAN

Amanda Jernigan

Interviewed by Ange Mlinko

A<small>MANDA</small> J<small>ERNIGAN IS THE AUTHOR</small> of two books of poems, *Groundwork* (Biblioasis, 2011) and *All the Daylight Hours* (Cormorant, 2013)—the first of these named to NPR's list of best books of the year—as well as of the monograph *Living in the Orchard: The Poetry of Peter Sanger* (Frog Hollow, 2014). She is the editor of *The Essential Richard Outram* (Porcupine's Quill, 2011) and, with Evan Jones, of *Earth and Heaven: An Anthology of Myth Poetry* (Fitzhenry & Whiteside, 2015). Her poems have appeared in *Poetry, Parnassus, PN Review, The Dark Horse, Atlanta Review,* and *The Nation,* as well as in numerous Canadian literary journals, and have been set to music. Jernigan is an essayist as well as a poet, and has written for the stage, collaborating with the members of DaPoPo Theatre in Halifax on the productions *Four Actors in Search of a Nation* and *Thirteen Ways of Looking at a Madman,* and on a public reading of her verse-play *Drinking Song.* She grew up in rural Ontario and lived for many years in Atlantic Canada, working as an editor, scholar, and teacher; she now lives in Hamilton, Ontario, with her husband—artist John Haney—and their two children.

◊ ◊ ◊ ◊

This interview was conducted over e-mail starting on Shakespeare's 452nd birthday—April 23, 2016—and completed on Midsummer Night, June 20, 2016.

AM: I'll say at the outset (and somewhat cheekily) that I dislike interviews. Not intrinsically, but because there are too many of them nowadays. They seem to have taken the place of serious reviewing or criticism. They're apt to domesticate or make diminutive (approachable, nonthreatening) their subjects. Where a good critic can enhance the mystique of a poet, interviewers (perhaps inadvertently) strip one of mystique.

AJ: I, too, dislike them, as Ms. Moore might say. For the reasons you note, among others. Though I love a good radio interview, with almost anyone: all the pleasures of eavesdropping (except the guilt), with none of the guilt. And there are some writers' interviews that I go back to, again and again. Richard Outram to Michael Carbert:

> Morality ultimately springs from faith. And the best definition of what I mean by that was articulated by Simone Weil when she said that "Faith is the experience of the intelligence illuminated by love." I can't think of it having been put any more cogently for my purposes. So through a morality springing from a faith of that nature and reflected through acts in the world, you can become imbued and endowed with an authority that vastly exceeds anything which you might accumulate through the power of might. Might is not right, though it may be dominant and dominate everything around it and ultimately may destroy everything, including all of its instruments. But authority is ultimately prior.

But, then, Outram was one of those people whose conversational speech actually enhanced rather than dispersed his mystique.

I think the Internet in general is disenchanting, to writers and to everything that comes within its virtual grasp, giving the illusion of accessibility to all: authors, Mars rovers, cave paintings, giraffes . . . My consolation is that this is, still, an illusion—the real world as intractable, as salutarily resistant, as ever. I hope.

AM: Your poems have mystique. They are powerful magical objects, and they would be so if we never knew anything about you.

AJ: I hope so. I hope, too, that poems have a kind of resistance: an ability to slough their authors and their authors' smalltalk as they move forward in time. George Johnston writes that poems aspire to the condition of anonymity. I think that's true.

AM: Nevertheless, here's the first disenchanting question: What was your education in poetry like? Did you have richly literate parents, or did you discover it in school; did you study it in university, or was there an alternate path?

AJ: I do have richly literate parents, both of them, though they are different sorts of readers. My mother is a literary editor: for thirty-some years she edited a well-known Canadian literary magazine called the *New Quarterly*, choosing fiction for its pages, and later commissioning a good deal of literary nonfiction, writing-about-writing, as well. And she, too, is born and bred in the briar patch: her father a newspaper man and occasional poet; her mother a scene-artist and costume designer manqué; her grandmother a woman of letters *avant la lettre,* who loved to read aloud. My father is an engineer and teacher, but he's the true "recreational reader" in our family, putting back the books, all sorts, at great speeds. And he's an avid cruciverbalist, as was his father before him. Both of my parents read aloud to me when I was young (still do, on occasion) and because I am the oldest in my family I got to hear the great books of my childhood (*Peter and Wendy, The Wind and the Willows, The Secret Garden, The Hobbit, The Yearling,* the *Narnia* books, *The Three Mulla-Mulgars, The Borrowers, The Racketty-Packetty House, Treasure Island, Charlotte's Web* . . .) more than once: first as they were read to me, and then as they were read to my sister and/or brother.

My maternal grandfather loved to read and recite poetry—Whittier, Longfellow, Riley; poems by Tennyson and Coleridge; Blake's "Tyger"; Hodgson's "Eve." I owe to him an ear for the accentual-syllabic meters that underlie my (English-language) speech—and also my sense of form not as an aberration of language, but as its foundation.

In my teenage years I read a lot of mid-twentieth-century Canadian poetry, with which the shelves of my high-school library were well stocked: the love lyrics of Leonard Cohen (I was drawn—well, to the love—but also to the song-structure that was implicit in his poetry, even before he took the show on the road) and Margaret Atwood (it was the mythopoeic aspect of her work that

attracted me). But I didn't really receive my *fiat* as a poet until later, when a university professor started giving us assignments like "write a sonnet," "write a villanelle." These were exercises, and to some extent we were meant to move beyond them. But they gave me license to draw from the well of my childhood listening, and I think I've never stopped. That said, I have avoided creative writing courses since then—the workshop environment being, for me, *deeply* disenchanting, however helpful I know it has been to some.

Then, too, the discovery of Outram's poetry, when I was in my early twenties, was hugely significant: here was a poet who strutted and fretted, his work full of linguistic brio, and unapologetically complex. Outram was from Southern Ontario, as was I; the place where he had grown up, now engulfed by Toronto, was a small town when he was a child there. I learned from him that a small-town Ontario girl (or boy) doesn't have to play dumb.

If one is interested in origins (and because, as you say, interviews, with their invitations to reflect on such matters, are thick on the ground), one can rehearse these things so often they become cliché. Rereading what I've written, two new facts occur:

First—and because we converse under the sign of the Bard (our interview begun on April 23rd)—I grew up twenty minutes down the road from the Stratford Festival, home to Canada's major Shakespeare company. My parents used to take me there, but also I went on school trips, by bus, rattling down gravel roads past pig farms to the theatre.

And I got to see some very fine productions, and to hear the beautiful language spoken aloud, by people who loved it.

And second: an education in poetry is more than an education in literature. So my father's delight in simple (and complex) math problems, and their solutions; a great aunt who taught me the names of tiny forest plants—these were probably as important as was Shakespeare.

AM: Can you say more about how you met Richard Outram, what your relationship was like, his position in Canadian poetry, and perhaps how you see your own position in Canadian poetry? It would be presumptuous of me to make any sweeping claims, but I do think of it as distinct from US poetry and from UK poetry. Can you tell me how that is, and why that is? Can you tell me, for instance, if you (and/or he) go with or against the grain?

AJ: I met Richard Outram and his wife, the artist Barbara Howard, quite coincidentally, through my mother-in-law. She is an environmental activist, and she shared with Outram and Howard an interest in, a concern for, whales and the oceans. Outram and Howard attended a fundraiser for whale scientists that my mother-in-law had organized. I spoke with them at the reception, and my husband (then my boyfriend: we were all of nineteen) offered them a ride to the closest subway station. I had discovered in conversation that Outram was a poet. I had never heard of him (testament more to my naiveté than to his critical neglect), for all that he had published twenty books.

Outram asked that evening for my address, saying that he would send me some poems. Which he did. And we corresponded for the next seven years, up until the time of his death (my last letter from him arriving after he was gone).

When I met Outram, I was fresh out of my first year of university—nursing writerly ambitions, but with little sense of what sort of a writer I might be. I was in a new relationship that was shaping up to be an enduring relationship, and there, too, I felt . . . scared: unsure of how to navigate the world in the context of the commitment it was increasingly evident my heart had made.

I have mentioned Outram's stylistic bravura—which did buck the trend of Canadian letters, especially coming out of the mid- to late-twentieth century, and which was exciting to me. But equally important was that I had the good luck to stumble upon one of the great English poets of committed, long-term love, just as I was stumbling into the relationship that would become my marriage. In Outram and Howard, I think John and I both came to see a model for a kind of life we might live: and learned something of how art-making, in the broadest sense, might be integral to that life.

The years since Outram's death now outnumber the years in which I knew him, so when I think about the effect that the relationship has had on me, I think as much about the absence as about the presence. I miss Outram. And I think about him a lot these days, as I work my way through his poems, which I'm editing for a collected edition: typing, proofreading, collating. In art there is a long tradition of learning by copying, and this can serve a poet, too. It builds one's muscles. It's a form of devotion. And it also builds in one the itch—perhaps, too, the ability—to do something that's radically one's own.

It's easier for me to talk about Outram's place in Canadian poetry than it is to talk about my own place. In 1988, the critic Alberto Manguel wrote:

> Until the 1960s, Canada barely acknowledged the existence of any Canadian literature. When, thanks to the perseverance of young writers such as Margaret Atwood, and stubborn editors such as Robert Weaver, readers made the discovery that this literature existed, the pantheon of authors chosen to represent it set a style against which the writing to come was measured. The most vociferous representatives of the newly discovered literature were poets, and small publishers of poetry—Anansi, Talonbooks, Coach House Press—were among its most energetic champions. In very broad terms, the style of what became recognized as Canadian poetry was simple-sounding, chatty, intimate but never overwhelmingly passionate, well-mannered, pleasantly funny, in obligatory free verse. . . . It is as if, in the beginning, Canadian literature chose to be easy. This, perhaps, explains why certain poets, Atwood included, are remembered for their lighter verse, and others whose work seems more complex are virtually ignored.

Outram—for Manguel "one of the finest poets in the English language"—was among the ignored.

The tenor of Canadian literature has changed since Manguel wrote this: in part because of Manguel and others like him (I think of Eric Ormsby and John Metcalf), with their wonderful, unapologetic cosmopolitanism. Then, too, there are homegrown canon-[re]shapers (Carmine Starnino, Jason Guriel, Zach Wells . . .), who have worked hard to teach Canadian readers (and writers) about the fascination of what's difficult. And equally important, the writers who have just continued to make obstinate, unfashionable work, sometimes in obscurity. (I think of M. Travis Lane and Peter Sanger, working away in Atlantic Canada, outside the circle of Toronto lit-light. Or the uncompromising minimalism of Souvankham Thammavongsa and Sean Howard. Or, in an earlier generation, Outram's contemporary, Jay Macpherson, whose work is important to me.) The literature is always more than gets noticed at any given time.

Which is one of the reasons a writer probably shouldn't be so foolish as to try to position herself within it!

Other people have written about my work in the context of feminist formalism, in a tradition of Canadian myth poetry, in relation to Outram's work, in the context of nature and ecology . . . But a poet's job is probably to pay as little attention as possible to such things, and to continue to follow her instincts in as unselfconscious a way as possible. If that's possible. (And, as that list betrays, it hasn't been, entirely, for me—though I try.)

I'm not well enough read in contemporary American or British poetry to say much about any differences, inherent or incidental, between what's going on here and what's going on south of the border, or across the pond. I did feel that, when I began to publish, I found a wider audience, sooner, in the States than I did in Canada. But that may have less to do with a different literary culture than it did with an accident of personalities. Christian Wiman at *Poetry* took poems of mine in 2005, when I'd published very little in Canada, and not at all in the States. Having read some of his work, now, I see reasons why my poems might have spoken to him. I consider it great good luck to have found such a reader.

AM: Do you read any foreign languages? Have you any foreign influences?

AJ: I am basically a monoglot. I have smatterings of Spanish, German, and Thai (I learned that last as a teenage exchange student, though my vocabulary is much eroded, now)—not enough to carry on a conversation; I can read French limpingly, with a dictionary. So my experience with poetry in languages other than English is almost entirely through translation: my *Odyssey* is Lattimore's *Odyssey;* my *Sonnets to Orpheus* are M.D. Herter Norton's *Sonnets to Orpheus;* my *Metamorphoses* is A.D. Melville's *Metamorphoses*... That said, certain translations (those ones, in particular) have been important to me.

AM: *Groundwork* suggests you studied archeology—am I right?

AJ: Yes, I did study archaeology. It's an old fascination: I used to dig up pill bottles and groundhog skulls on the river bank behind my parents' house. My university offered courses in Classics, which I took until I got spooked by the language requirement (I regret, now, that I didn't learn Latin and Greek)—and a summer field school, working on a dig in North Africa. I loved the field work. The scholarship I found, in its minutiae, less interesting, so I schlepped off to the English department.

But there is something archaeological about my work, still—the work on Outram, say. The whole impossible, necessary business of trying to bring the past to light.

Archaeological, and mythological: Outram's papers are held at the Thomas Fisher Rare Book Library in Toronto. To access the collection you go up three flight of stairs, then into a Stygian lobby, where you divest yourself of anything with pockets. An elevator takes you down a story to the reading room. So there is a sense of descent to an underworld—even though the reading room windows look out onto the street, with its incongruous spectacle of backpacked students on their ways.

AM: "The literature is always more than gets noticed at any given time."—That's a lovely way to put it. And while I agree that it is, on the whole, not terribly useful to think of oneself as "positioned" in the field, I ask because there's a stance toward time inherent in it. Your poems take into account different kinds of time—planetary, mythical, historical—and the stories you tell often feel of another time, or even completely outside of time. This is accomplished through the masks of literary characters such as Lear or Odysseus (I absolutely adore "Islands"), but some you seem to have invented (I'm thinking of, for example, "The Marble King of Athens, Greece"—where in the world did that come from? Or "Favourite"). You do interleave *All the Daylight Hours* with tender personal poems, whose "I" is recognizable as yourself, frequently addressed to loved ones, in lived time. But on balance, your collections do not pitch themselves in secular or "ordinary time" (to use a phrase I used to read as a child in weekly Mass leaflets). Even your account of your friendship with Richard Outram seems of a piece with the idea that time is long and deep and cyclical rather than linear—and he was, unbeknownst to you, showing you your future.

So this led me to wonder if you think at all about the pressures and imperatives to write about the here and now. There is a hysterical insistence that poets be "relevant," that is, write in response to news headlines. I think poets are enslaved by the contemporary— one's contemporaries—yet I also believe in criticism, in discourse. And if this tips my hand a bit, I'm also thinking of your biting little poem, "On Modern Verse," which does betray a hint of animosity towards the contemporary.

AJ: There's a lot here I could speak to.

I am a country mouse living in the city, and although I've learned to walk without constantly looking over my shoulder, I'm not really naturalized to urban life. A lot of what's around me seems unreal: all this industrialized infrastructure, from the crosswalks to the government buildings to the billboards for personal injury lawyers (ubiquitous in Hamilton, for some reason)— to say nothing of the steel mills—a kind of aberration. Not that I hate it—there is a lot to like about living in a city, and this is home to me; indeed, I've come to love it, in a kind of family way. And I'm deeply dependent on it. But it does still seem to me a bit . . . illusory. And then, this is the other thing: a lot of it is illusory, or had better be, if we're going to survive as a species. Not that we can't have cities: most of us live in cities. But we need to figure out radically new ways to live in them. To look after each other in them. And to *be*, on the face of this planet, whether urban or rural. When I think about being "relevant," I think about writing poems that will still be relevant, when the ivory cities fall. To put it apocalyptically. (And lest I make myself out to be a complete urbanophobe: what I'm really talking about isn't urban life but consumer culture. And capitalism, in all its rapacious ugliness. Which struts and frets more loudly in cities than it does outside of them: "Prepare for death by banking your assets with TLC," "Spring is home-improvement time," "Begin a new life with LaserPeeps" . . .)

But there's an ethical imperative, too, to writing about the world as we know it. I certainly don't write for some kind of post-human future: who would want to do this, even if it were possible (and it's not, in the beautiful, human artifact and living entity that is language). No. I am deeply in love with humanity, and I write for humanity, and in the faith that, in spite of much evidence to the contrary, we are worth saving. "Love calls us to the things of this world," says Richard Wilbur, and that's true. And I admire a writer like my countryman Steven Heighton, whose poems take in a broad sweep of history yet also caressingly embrace the dailiness of "writing cheques or checking e-mail."

But I think often of Northrop Frye's distinction between primary concerns (food, sex, shelter, liberty of movement [I'd add love, in its many forms]) and secondary concerns (patriotism, religion, class-conditioned attitudes and behaviors). "All through history secondary concerns have taken precedence over primary ones," he writes. "We want to live, but we go to war; we want freedom, but permit, in varying degrees of complacency, an immense amount of exploitation, of ourselves as well as of others; we want happiness, but allow most of our lives to go to waste. The twentieth century [and how much more is this true of the twenty-first], with its nuclear weaponry and its pollution that threatens the supply of air to breathe and water to drink, may be the first time in history when it is really obvious that primary concerns must become primary, or else." Frye makes it clear that there isn't any golden age before the rise of secondary concern that we can hearken back to. And I don't mean to idealize the pre-industrial past. I am keenly aware of the fact that, especially as a woman, I'd be much worse off in almost any other time and place than the one I am fortunate to

inhabit. But more and more, what I want to write about is primary concern.

You mention personae: I wanted to be an actor before I wanted to be a writer, so this mask-making is in part a way to live that dream by other means. And of course masks can signify different aspects of the self, as well as signifying others. Both these aspects of mask-making are important, I think: the aspect of it that emphasizes the distinctness of self and other, and the aspect of it that emphasizes their identity. I love performance, and the plasticity of identity in performance. And the ability to command, in writing, an androgynous voice: or, rather, one that can move along the spectrum of gender. And be young or old, human or (anthropomorphized) animal. What Empedocles said about pre-incarnation rings true for me, about the inner life: "For already have I once been a boy and a girl, a bush and a bird and a dumb sea fish." (But then, too, I love the surprise one gets from life, when one realizes that however much one has acted the part, one hasn't come close to understanding the real thing. Thus, for instance—for me—motherhood. But that's another kettle of fry.)

In keeping with the maxim that truth is stranger than fiction, both "The Marble King" and the woman in "Favourite" are based, albeit loosely, on people in my life.

There are two more strands in what you say that I want to tease out.

First of all, criticism, discourse. Yes. I love to read good literary criticism. But I tend to go more for books or published magazines, on or off-line, than for blogs (with a couple of exceptions). Finding the Internet a rabbit hole. And there's a big difference, for me, between "criticism, discourse," and the kind of tweetable sniping (see "On Modern Verse") that so often goes on online. I think a writer is well out of the latter.

I've always haunted the mailbox, waiting for its daily possible tidings of the outside world. E-mail is a mailbox that can cough up a missive at any time, and for that reason it's a terrible, constant distraction. For that reason, too, I don't "do" social media at all: that would be the end of me.

But finally: circling back to what you say about time. Yes: time, change, that's the great subject. It's time that robs us of everything we have. On the other hand, it's time that gives us everything we have, and that is the container for everything we have.

Time, and memory, which is our container for time.

AM: I'd like to end on something a little lighter, so here are two final questions. First: I would love to know if you, as coeditor of *Earth and Heaven: An Anthology of Myth Poetry,* have a favorite myth.

AJ: I don't have a particular favorite myth, but rather a series of myths that have spoken to my condition at various times—and a fascination, too, with the way the unfolding of experience can open different stories to our understanding, and vice versa, as we go along. When I was in my peripatetic twenties, I thought a lot about the *Odyssey*—also the initial stories of Genesis, with their reflections on beginnings and on relationships, personal, creative, and ecological. Now, in my thirties,

with children, I think of the Christian stories of Annunciation and Nativity, and, in the Classical tradition, of various mothers: Callisto and Demeter, centrally, for me. And I think that for a poet, stories of makers, and Makers, will be perennially important. Orpheus, Arachne. God.

AM: Okay, and second: I would love it if you could tell me a) What place you've always wanted to visit but never have; and b) What your favorite salad is. (I think of salad as the food most like to poetry—the greatest variety or texture in a space of containment!)

AJ: I had the good fortune to travel a lot when I was younger: a year in Thailand, as I mentioned; that summer working in North Africa; shorter trips to Berlin, to southern Spain, to the UK, and to Ecuador, where my sister briefly lived. That was a wealth of experience, and a well of trouble, too, and there are ways in which I think I'm still recovering—and, on the other hand, still reveling in the settled glories of home. I'm aware, too, that at the age of thirty-seven I've already burned through more fossil fuels than any human being has a right to. So I think more of road trips, than of plane trips (not that road trips are carbon-innocent!). Whitehorse, in the Yukon: a road not taken, from my twenties. Marianna, Arkansas, where my great-grandfather, proprietor of a diner, purportedly made forty pies a day . . .

As for favorite salad: that's easy. My husband, John, *il miglior fabbro,* makes the best Caesar salad known to Man. Or at least to Amanda.

Amanda Jernigan

Little Boy Blue

Lost in the corn, the story goes,
a child or poet could unlose
herself by following the rows
which, every schoolgirl knows,
end at the margin: verse ain't prose—

or so I thought. And so I chose
to enter. It is green here, crow's-
eye-view relinquished: bees,
unlost, malinger; yellow flowers
only the detasseler sees.

And yet, although the whole field bows,
the leaves cathedralling the rows
above the walker, the stalks close
ranks; my entrypoint withdraws
beyond refinding; countless days

have passed uncounted; I am lazy
with the heat. The art of losing
isn't hard to master: it betrays
one into thinking it is all there is.

Amanda Jernigan

Final Correspondence, on a Gallery Notecard

(A detail from a marginal decoration in the Luttrell Psalter)

Still stricken by your glyph, I flip
the card (the Magi, on the verso,
are engaged in conversation), rehearse,
again, as they must, the significance
of their gifts, passing the long hours
of their journey: gold, and frankincense, and myrrh,
and gold, and frankincense, and myrrh, and gold . . .

Their ragamuffin horses are unhurried.
But neither do they turn and they
have carried me a decade forth
in time from when you trusted this
to post, back in the short days
of another year, and look
around us, Richard, there are children.

Amanda Jernigan

Nativities

I   After the angels have gone home,
           the baby sleeps. What does he dream?
           The night, before the world began?
           The world? Or his creation, Man?
           The wise men wonder. It will keep.
           The baby nurses in his sleep.

II   Yes, Frye, I have heard the angels singing,
           and I tell you, pace Eliot, they did sing to me
           (though human voices raised to chant
           the son of God will always drown
           out the voices of angels sent
           to earth to chant the son of man).

III   The baby came out screaming fit
           to wake the stone-deaf dead, forget
           the living: a gut-wrenched, lonely,
           livid wail—a sound that only
           a mother could love, if not quite hear
           as choirs of heavenly angels, here.

Amanda Jernigan

The Oracle, Retired

Truth-telling, I tell you
(and once that would have been
God's truth, or mine,
it was the same back
then), is a young
person's game. Not
that you lose the knack;
you lose the taste:
you come to find the whole
cold hard caboodle
an expense of spirit in a waste
of shame. The ring
becomes a rattle; you shy
from firsts and lasts and fly
to middles; and you lie
awake at night
worrying the riddles:
truth-telling is a young
person's game.

Amanda Jernigan

Burning the Love Letters

for Richard Outram and Barbara Howard

Given on first reading
to feed

the flames of early
love, they're burning,

now, redundantly, but still give heat,
and we congratulate

ourselves on being
here—still here, still we—

to feel it,
to watch those words turned flesh turn flame again until

you turn to me: *it's nice—*
who burn their love letters warm themselves twice.

Amanda Jernigan

Promissory Note

Hickory dickory dock,
the mouse ran up the clock:
while he is there, pull up a chair,
and you and I can talk,

and tire the sun with talking
and send him down the sky,
discussing ships and sealing wax
and whether we will die,

and how to pick a lock,
and the collective noun
for basilisks—the mouse ran down.
Hickory dickory dock.

Amanda Jernigan

Counting Rhyme

Stone cold, age of gold;
gilded salver, age of silver;
brain, brawn: age of bronze;
hoar briar, age of iron;
ore-stain, age of stone;
some one: age of bone;
bonefish: age of flesh;
flash flood, age of wood;
still birth: age of earth.

Timothy Reilly

Every Other Friday

— For Jo-Anne

KEN DELANEY HAD TO EASE ME IN on his secret. He needed to be able to trust me. He began by asking if I ever felt my parents were strangers.

"I never thought about them that way," I said.

"Think about it a minute," he said. "Just think about it."

I thought about it. I was simultaneously looking inside myself and outward at the distant San Gabriel Mountains and the thunderheads looming above them. The world suddenly expanded and became lonelier and more threatening.

"I think I see what you mean," I said, with a hint of awe.

We were heading north, walking on the left side of a road bordering an orange grove.

It was getting hotter, so we entered the grove, picked a couple of oranges, and sat under a wind-break eucalyptus. We ate our oranges, talked about girls, and then continued our trek through the orange grove, until we came to a stretch that had been leveled by chain saws and bulldozers. The local state college was making way for new buildings and parking lots. It looked like No Man's Land. A year ago we would have grabbed some rifle-size sticks and played army, but we were now too old for that kind of thing: we were about to enter the eighth grade.

Ken sat down on a tree stump and threw dirt clods at a resting tractor. "I want to tell you something," he said without looking at me. "But you have to promise not to tell anyone else."

115

"Okay. I promise."

"I was born on another planet." He sounded serious.

"What planet?" I asked.

"I'm not sure. I was real young when they abandoned me here. But I think I came from Mars."

We discussed all the planets in our solar system, and agreed that Mars was the most reasonable candidate. We ruled out light-speed transportation.

"Can you remember any canals?" I asked.

He shook his head.

THAT EVENING, AT THE DINNER TABLE, I studied my parents' faces. The resemblance I bore to them seemed insignificant: perhaps even accidental. Who were these people? Why was I with them? I weighed what Ken had told me about his birthright. Was it possible we shared the same home-planet? Or could he have been pulling my leg?

I thought back to my third grade classmate, Jimmy Schneider, who had once tricked me into looking for miniature dinosaurs in the cornfield bordering the school playground. I never really believed Jimmy's story. I knew that the footprints he'd pointed out to me were raven tracks—not the wanderings of a pint-sized Tyrannosaurus rex. Nevertheless, I followed Jimmy, at recess, under the chain link fence, into the cornfield, and later into the principal's office, for my first and only school paddling.

But that was kid's stuff, willing make-believe. Ken was neither a liar nor a practical joker. His confession was earnest and

disturbing and strangely credible. It made me think back even further: to when I was five or six. I had certain thoughts then—creepy thoughts—that seemed to come from somewhere outside my own making. I somehow got the notion that everyone on the planet was putting me on; that when they left a room, they would go to some secret place to compare notes and plan the next illusion for keeping me in the dark. The play was all for my benefit; everything that happened was only performance, props and acting, and the real world—whatever that was—would always be in another place, just beyond my reach.

"Why aren't you eating?" my mother broke through my thoughts. Her timing was scary. "Have you been eating those malt balls again? I told you not to eat those things before dinner."

"I didn't have any malt balls."

"What, then? Are you sick? Let me feel your forehead."

The following morning, I walked the four blocks to Ken's house. I normally would have met him on the sidewalk, but today I was anxious to tell him my revelation: that I, too, was of Martian blood. I rang the doorbell.

Mrs. Delaney answered the door and I introduced myself. She called out for Ken and then asked if I'd like some cookies. She seemed very pleasant. When Ken arrived she said she would put some Oreos out on the kitchen table.

"Just leave us alone," Ken sneered at his mother. "Stay out of my life."

I was dumbstruck. I had never heard anyone talk to his mother that way—leastwise, not in front of company. Mrs. Delaney's face

116

turned deep red. Her eyes welled and her mouth tightened to a shriveled scar. I half-expected her to slap Ken's unguarded face, but she instead hurried from the room.

Ken instructed me to follow him down a hallway, as if I were a client with an appointment.

He shared a bedroom with his older brother, Dom. As I entered the room, I noticed a small holy water font next to the light switch—just like the holy water font in my own bedroom. Out of habit, we both dipped our fingers and crossed ourselves. I saw nothing of the penitent in Ken's face. A German Mauser hung above the door: a trophy, I was told, from their father's participation in the Second World War. Not to be outdone, I mentioned my dad's Nazi helmet and bayonet. "The helmet has a bullet hole in it," I said.

Three of their bedroom walls were decorated with college pennants and pictures of Sandy Koufax, Sophia Loren, the Mercury astronauts, and the official White House portrait of Kennedy: in which the President sits at his desk, looking up from a stack of papers. Kennedy was my hero. I admired his wit and courage and intelligence. But for some reason, the look on his face in this portrait troubled me. I couldn't tell whether he was about to smile or was perturbed at being interrupted from his reading.

A small crucifix had its own uncluttered space above Ken and Dom's bunk beds. It was a graphic representation of the crucified Christ: with parchment-colored skin and bright-red blood streaming from His wounds.

My older brother and I no longer shared a room, but I had always wanted bunk beds.

I thought it would be manly to climb aloft to sleep. Dom now sat atop his bunk reading a book. He seemed a more handsome version of his younger brother. I decided not to mention anything Martian, unless Ken gave the okay.

"What are you reading?" I asked Dom.

"*War of the Worlds,* by H.G. Wells," he said. "Have you read it?"

"I saw the movie."

"No comparison."

Ken showed no interest in the topic. He suggested we play three-way burnout in the backyard. He lent me a decent fielder's glove.

The brothers threw the hardball at each other with much more velocity than when they threw to me. There was for awhile a silent tension between the two, until Dom spoke out.

"You shouldn't talk to Linda the way you do," he said to Ken. "She's been real kind to us."

"She's a bitch," Ken said.

"Don't say that."

"She's a dumb bitch and I hate her guts."

The brothers threw down their gloves and slowly approached each other, as if in the preliminaries of a duel. A short pushing match ensued and Dom took Ken to the lawn in a legal wrestling hold. It was impressive. Both boys were in top physical shape (I had noticed a 125 pounds set of weights on their patio). No punches were thrown—it was all formal wrestling. Ken fought bravely but he was no match for his older brother, who had pinned Ken's arms with his knees and begun a round of Chinese water torture: the relentless metronomic poke of the index finger into the sternum.

"Take it back," said Dom. Tap-tap-tap-tap . . .

"She's a dumb bitch and I hate her guts," Ken persisted.

"Take it back." Tap-tap-tap-tap . . . "Say uncle." Tap-tap-tap-tap-tap-tap . . .

Ken seemed willing to die rather than surrender. Dom did not have the killer instinct. The match ended in an uncertain draw.

Later that day I asked Ken who Linda was.

"She's supposed to be my stepmother, but she's nothing. She's a dumb bitch and I hate her guts."

That was all he would say about the woman who had offered me Oreos. Martian citizenship would also become a dead topic.

When I got home that afternoon, my mother told me she had spoken on the telephone with Mrs. Delaney. "We had a long talk," she said. "Mrs. Delaney said you have good manners."

I didn't know how to respond. I didn't want to betray my friend by taking the side of his enemy. But then I surprised myself. I did something I hadn't done in a long time: I confided in my mother.

"She's Ken's stepmother, actually," I said. "He hates her. I can't understand why; she seems really nice."

"She *is* really nice," my mother said. "But try to be understanding with Ken. Be patient. Think about what it would be like if *I* died. I would hope you would think that no one else could replace me. Because it's true. We're not furniture. We can't be replaced. Ken is dealing with something impossible

to comprehend: the early death of a parent. Right now, anger is the only way he can express his grief. He'll find better ways as he gets older."

I was taken aback by my mother's show of intelligence and compassion. I had no idea.

That night, sleep came in small doses. I was attacked from all angles by the dark and persistent thought of losing my own mother. I tried to suppress the thought, but it was no use: I was paying the penalty for knowledge.

In the morning I walked to Ken's house. We got on the topic of our upcoming confirmations. We had both chosen the names of saints who had not been martyred. We favored the idea of leading a holy life without dismemberment or violent death. I chose St. Patrick. I admired his courage and faith and power of persuasion. I loved the legends surrounding him and the fact that he was the patron saint of Ireland: the land of my ancestors.

"You do know that he never really chased out any snakes, don't you?" Ken quizzed me.

"Of course," I said. "The snakes were a—what-do-ya-call-it."

"A metaphor."

"Yeah. The snakes represent evil, the devil . . . things like that."

Ken said he had picked St. Augustine. He liked the fact that Augustine had written great books and had led an adventurous life that included several girlfriends. "He was one of the smartest men who ever lived," Ken said. He also confessed that he wanted to be able to use "Gus" for a nickname.

118

Later in the day, as we were playing a game of Yahtzee, Ken fell into one of his silent moods.

"What's wrong?" I asked.

"My dad and the Bitch said they were going to send me to a Catholic junior high."

"Why?"

He shrugged his shoulders resignedly. He then suggested we walk to the TG&Y so he could buy a kit model of *The Wolf Man*. "You can paint the legs," he said.

During dinner, my mother mentioned that she had again been on the telephone with Mrs. Delaney, and that the two of them came up with a plan to help Ken and me keep in touch—even though we'd be going to different schools. The plan was to set aside every other Friday, for a shared recreation. It could be a movie or miniature golf or something else—the choice would be ours.

For the first of our Friday outings, we chose the Balboa Fun Zone. Mrs. Delaney drove us through Balboa Island and onto the ferry for a three-minute boat ride to the Fun Zone. *Island* is a generous term for this platter of soil connected to the mainland by a bridge the length of a driveway. Balboa Island consists of a tiny downtown and web of narrow streets with houses and shops crammed together like pieces on a Monopoly game board. But the ferry ride to the Fun Zone made me feel like a sailor headed for a raucous shore-leave in an exotic foreign port.

It was the last weekend before the start of a new school year, and the Fun Zone was packed. First thing we did was ride the Ferris wheel. We bought frozen bananas, checked out the girls, hit the penny arcade, and bought some souvenir novelties. When we got back home, Mrs. Delaney prepared us a dinner of cheese toasties and tomato soup. We ended up in the brothers' bedroom: comparing our souvenirs and observations.

"Friday after next, I'll kick your butt in miniature golf," said Ken.

Dom suggested that the next time we should instead ask to be taken to Knott's Berry Farm. "It doesn't cost anything to get in. You can spend time at the old-fashioned penny arcade, walk around the lagoon and the Ghost Town . . . drink boysenberry juice. You can watch *real* cancan girls at the Calico Saloon—that's the best." He showed us the garter belt he'd once caught from a Calico Saloon cancan girl. He kept it slung around his top bunk bedpost. "She tossed it right to me," he said.

"Bullshit," Ken said. "She just threw it without even looking."

"She looked me right in the eyes and tossed it to me. She chose me."

"Can I see it?" I said.

Dom twirled the belt around his index finger then let it fly down to me. I dropped it.

"You better be able to catch it, if a cancan girl tosses one to you," said Dom.

"Maybe we should go to Knott's Berry Farm, next time," I said to Ken.

"We already decided to go miniature golfing."

"Well, then, how about the time after that?"

"Okay. Knott's Berry Farm after miniature golf."

The Knott's Berry Farm adventure would be pushed ahead one more time. My mother insisted on taking us to see *It's a Mad, Mad, Mad, Mad World*. "It won't be here next week," she said, "so we'd better see it now."

Ken and I were glad we saw the movie; every comedian in the world was in it. The Three Stooges even made a cameo appearance.

Two weeks later, we were finally set to go to Knott's Berry Farm. Mrs. Delaney would drop us off and then pick us up at closing time. We would be left on our own. We were now officially "teenagers."

At school that day, my mind was far from the curriculum. Most of the students in my afternoon social studies class were suffering from a similar brand of yearning. A combination of hormones and the celebratory mood of Friday made all of us anxious and scatterbrained. Mrs. Ford's lecture reached my ears as a mere humming noise. I was thinking about boysenberry juice and garter belts.

"And what do you think about that?" said Mrs. Ford, suddenly standing before my desk.

"It's difficult to say," I said, as if I'd been listening.

She looked at me long enough to let me know she was on to me. "I'll bet," she said at last.

It took me no time to retreat back into my head, where my thoughts continued to bounce between the mundane and the adolescent erotic. I meditated on Gerald Jacob's cowlick: how it formed a perfect question mark. I did my best in imagining certain girls naked. I marveled at Steven Knoll's ability to decorate the blank areas of his Pee Chee folder with accurate drawings of tanks, diving Messerschmitts, and the bolt-action rifles used in the Second World War. I dreaded the looming threat of fish-sticks for dinner.

I was off somewhere in the middle of a heroic daydream when Joe Looney tapped me on the back of the head and whispered that he could see Lorrie Easley's nipples when she bent over to get something from under her desk.

I couldn't see a thing.

Just then, a faceless boy entered the classroom and said that the radio was on in his woodshop class and some guy had interrupted the music to say that President Kennedy had been shot.

The whole class made a clipped gasping noise: like a huge machine coming to an abrupt halt.

"Mr. Swanson wanted me to tell you," the boy said, as if offering an excuse or apology.

Mrs. Ford began to say something but rushed from the room before she could finish. A long silence held, until the principal's quivering voice reported over the intercom the news from Dallas.

To this day I can remember every detail of President Kennedy's televised funeral—the empty saddle, my family weeping, the steadfast cadence of tenor drums, the Irish Cadets at the gravesite—but I remember very little from the principal's confirmation of the President's death. I remember only that I had been set adrift in a classroom full of people my own age, and that none of us knew what to do next.

Catharine Savage Brosman

Trumpet Vine

Chromatic fanfares in the garden flash—
nasturtiums, dahlias, phlox, blue columbine—
around the feet of pine and mountain ash,
antiphonally with a trumpet vine,

which, by its adventitious rootage, climbs,
displaying pennate leafage: emerald green
when new, then later dark; vermilion cymes
with yellow throats articulate the scene.

It's *Campsis radicans,* though; suckers spread
and propagate their kind with greedy ease.
Thus woody growth, unpruned, can get ahead
of us and strangle hospitable trees.

No matter now; that garden is a ghost—
a vital plant become a paradigm
of death; perennials gone; a fallen host;
the horticulturist choked off by time.

Philosophy does not suffice; one needs
fresh laughter, mountain air, the scent of pine,
the flowers of remembrance, even weeds,
to match the high notes of the trumpet vine.

Jeanne Emmons

Packing Daddy's Books

He never gave a book away. He hoarded
as only a child of the Depression could,
who, at twelve, on winter nights, had stood
before the shelf on which his mother stored
her Tennyson, her Browning and Defoe
beside the jars of succotash and greens.
His forefinger would tip back *Ivanhoe*,
careful not to disturb the peas, the beans.
He'd find a chair, hunch over his dreams.

In forty years of teaching he amassed
enough for a third world of starved minds.
Retired, he brought them all home. They lined
every shelf, then immigrated past
the living room and study to the closets,
the empty bedrooms of the grown children.
He'd reread one, or, thinking he'd lost it,
buy it again. We joked that they would spawn
and overpopulate, spill onto the lawn.

His legs failed. He paged through catalogues
and ordered by the score. Towers rose up,
whole civilizations on tables, chairs, a trunk,
the fireplace ledge. All day he'd scorn and slog
through page after page, penciling in the margins.
And, when his memory went, he underlined
each sentence, heavily, as if, to his mind,
every thought were enormously important,
every syllable a wall against disorder.

At the last, his books grew silent of him.
He might spend hours on a single paragraph.
I think he found some comfort in the form
of the characters lined up like a dark path
on which his eyes could march from left to right,
and make that turn and then go right again.
The simple look of it, the black on white,
and thicker white on all four sides, and then,
more blank and open white at chapter's end.

At last, we boxed them up. We made no judgments.
Spy stories, physics, medieval romance,
Bible commentaries, a book on the Luddites,
the Klan, yoga, ninjas, modern dance
—all in cartons to settle their resentments
like Greeks and Trojans, merciless, no regrets
(Daddy out of the fray, sulking in his tent)
. . . or still as lovers in the tombs of the Capulets.

Doris Watts

Fear of Forgetting

Something drops, slips,
falls—to the surface first,
then below, turning, tips,
sinks, as if into stirred
water, turbulent,
and so one finds oneself
reaching after it, intent
now on nothing else

but its rescue
before it joins the rest
at the bottom, lost,
indistinguishable—
coin, leaf, pebble,
your face, your name, you.

John Ellis

A Review of Clive James, *Sentenced to Life*

New York, New York: Liveright Publishing Corporation, 2016

ISBN 978-1-63149-172-6, 80 pp., USA $24.95, hardcover

★ ★ ★

AUTHOR AND POET CLIVE JAMES' *Sentenced to Life* is a somber retrospective in the face of illness and aging. Now seventy-six, James has survived a battle with leukemia, and he muses over his existence and the day-to-day routines of managing medication, senility, and memories.

Throughout, James reports the exertion of penning verse in his infirm state. In his mind, "the fires are dying fast"; a single page of double-spaced poetry takes him half the day to compose. The collection is nonetheless a vibrant display of James' prowess as a poet as well as his propensity toward seemingly effortless meter and rhyme; the majority of it moves in stanzas that embody unforced rhyme scheme, natural and well-crafted at the same time:

> My sin was to be faithless. I would lie
> As if I could be true to everyone
> At once, and all the damage that was done
> Was in the name of love, or so I thought.
> I might have met my death believing this,
> But no, there was a lesson to be taught.

There are several departures from this, but they make for comfortable variation. Meter and rhyme is a key ingredient in James' previous collections as well; perhaps because he has had so much practice, James' sense of organic word pairings is unparalleled here.

In addition, the collection straddles a line between solipsistic and universally accessible as it asks what life is in the face of death. One wonders if *Sentenced to Life,* so starkly honest, borders too closely on the elegiac; the reader seems always on the verge of becoming a participant in James' funeral song.

From the moment one sees the cover image of a falling Japanese maple leaf, the collection's thematic intentions—autumn, decline, inevitable winter—are made clear. Titles such as "Procedure for Disposal" and "Managing Anger" are the first to signal the poems' saturnine fixations, and on closer inspection, much of the material is obsessed with analogizing such things. Fraught with the deliberations of one staring down his own mortality, James speaks candidly in the confessional tradition. The figure of discourse changes throughout: sometimes it addresses the reader, sometimes the general audience, and sometimes a family member. In the case of the first, one feels as if he or she sits in vigil at James' bedside, in dialogue with a man reeling in despondency, indignation, and, occasionally, gratitude.

In "Manly Ferry," figurative language predominates as James compares himself to the *South Steyne,* a boat not yet decommissioned or, as in "Driftwood Houses," to makeshift sandcastles on the beach, ready for the tide. James has maintained a reputation as a polymath, and in addition to his rampant use of metaphor, the material is, more often than not, allusive, with tangential references to literature, film, history, political figures, current events, and popular culture. The material forms a kind of ecclesiastical reverie as James makes an account of his own finite nature, and thematically this makes the collection largely monotone—many of the poems begin and end in fits of melancholy. There are several unexpected breaks in sobriety, however: One prose poem describes a South African Safari ("One Elephant, Two Elephant"); there is a deliberation over a mobster's assassination ("Bugsy Siegel's Flying Eye"); and a lascivious scene follows a Russian Ballet ("Only the Immortal Need Apply"). While these might be welcome respites from James' heavier introspections, they appear strangely positioned against the book's major refrain—coping with the day to day.

In "Landfall," James considers how he

> once was free
> From pills in heaps, blood tests, X-rays and scans.
> No pipes or tubes. At perfect liberty,
> I stained my diary with travel plans.

One might be caught off guard by the reoccurring depiction of tedium; indeed, the initial third of the book is monotone in that regard. But James' verse is also punctuated by more sanguine realizations:

Today I am restored by my decline
And by the harsh awakening it brings.
I was born weak and always have been weak.

For James, the act of writing is both a catharsis and a tool for contrast. Youth and vanity are juxtaposed with the years of "posing like the statue of a man in pain" as he puts it in "My Home." The visceral reality of his condition is apparent in lines like "Grasping at straws, I bless another day/ Of having felt not much less than all right." In "Holding Court," James describes the effort it takes to maintain a discussion: "With conversation, I don't try to guess/ At meanings, or unpack a stroke of wit,/ But just send silent signals with my face/ That claim I've not succumbed to loneliness." Lines like these are bandied with James' memories, creating an ever more dramatic tension between what James had and what he is continuing to lose. He also paints beautiful albeit morbid images throughout, such as when he envisions his death, a "sudden and convulsive showdown." In the first portion of the collection, these images rarely abate, and when they do it's only briefly and in lieu of very different topics. In "Nature Programme," James begins by describing the wiles of certain species' mating habits or birds training for flight. The poem eventually transitions into more familiar territory as James describes the wiles of tiger sharks that lie in wait for albatross chicks "doomed to the atrophy of lust"; he concludes the poem with the foreboding "They could be you:/ Wonder of nature that you were."

Arguably, James' methods are at their best when he gives his reader a glimpse of grandeur; in spite of the sometimes overwhelming melancholy of the collection, it nods at the power of life in spite of oppression. For example, in "My Home," James states, "We fade away, but vivid in our eyes/ A world is born again that never dies." There is a powerful duality here, as James describes something sovereign beyond his mortality. Contrast this with the image in "Living Doll" of an Aufstehpuppe, a rebalancing puppet that sits in James' living room. While the puppet always recovers to a straightened position, James is nothing like it since he is a man who has been knocked askew and can't recover. He returns to imploring the reader to realize the inevitable, life laid bare in all its misery: "Of how we are defeated in the end," he says of the doll passing to a family member once he is deceased, "But still begin again in the new lives/ Which sort our junk, deciding what to keep./ Let them keep this, a cheap doll that contrives/ To stand straight even as I fall asleep."

Towards the book's center, there is a departure from death, senility, and remembrance; this is where James begins to fall short. His recollections of a life long-lived take a hiatus in favor of poems like "Nina Kogan's Geometrical Heaven" and "Asma Unpacks Her Pretty Clothes." These poems, although fantastic by any measure, seem misplaced, dropped in from somewhere outside this collection. This is not only because they lack cohesion with the book's major themes but also because several of them retreat from James' traditional form. "One Elephant, Two Elephant," is an example of both of these deviations, as it proceeds in the elongated and conversational trek of a prose poem that recounts a safari. The aforementioned two poems embody James' more traditional form, but their subjects are a noticeable break from the book's sobering undercurrent. Occasionally, James is unabashedly funny too, and when he is, it seems to come out of left field. Perhaps diversity is what James intended—these are, after all, poems amassed from a specific four-year period—but these exceptions give the appearance of having been included merely to fatten the collection; they are starkly out of place.

Inevitably, James returns to the familiar; his overarching desire for the introspection of years is too much to ignore. In the latter half of the collection, everything from a night sky ("Star Systems") to the process of changing homes ("Change of Domicile") invokes an exploration of decline, death, and all things in between. There is the incessant bereavement over the loss of a loved one and the inevitable loss of oneself, and James laments the latter in the former poem,

> Perhaps an old man dying would do well
> To smile as he rejoins the cosmic dust
> Life comes from, for resign himself he must.

One recalls the cover image of the Japanese maple leaf wafting softly in the breeze and wonders if it would have been more appropriate raging against a hurricane.

While *Sentenced to Life* may not be elevated to the level of Lamentations or Job, the book is laudable for its introspection and pathos. These are especially apparent as James recounts his past, a life, according to him, long-gone but not long-forgotten. It is then that the collection echoes the sweetness of blissful remembrances and the inevitable tranquility that accompanies the certainty of one's passing. As James so appropriately concludes in "Rounded with a Sleep," "My death is something I must live with now."

Able M U S E
A REVIEW OF POETRY, PROSE & ART

*After more than a decade of online publishing excellence,
Able Muse began a bold new chapter with its Print Edition*

**We continue to bring you in print the usual
masterful craft with poetry, fiction, essays,
art & photography, and book reviews**

Check out our 12+ years of online archives for work by

RACHEL HADAS • X.J. KENNEDY • TIMOTHY STEELE • MARK JARMAN • A.E.
STALLINGS • DICK DAVIS • A.M. JUSTER • TIMOTHY MURPHY • DEBORAH
WARREN • CHELSEA RATHBURN • RHINA P. ESPAILLAT • TURNER CASSITY •
RICHARD MOORE • STEPHEN EDGAR • ANNIE FINCH • THAISA FRANK •
NINA SCHUYLER • SOLITAIRE MILES • MISHA GORDIN • & SEVERAL OTHERS

SUBSCRIPTION
Able Muse – Print Edition – Subscriptions:

Able Muse is published semiannually.

Subscription rates—for individuals: $28.00 per year; single and previous issues: $19.95 + $3 S&H.

International subscription rates: $35 per year; single and previous issues: $19.95 + $5 S&H.
(All rates in USD.)

Subscribe online with WePay/credit card **www.ablemusepress.com**

Or send a check payable to *Able Muse Review*
Attn: Alex Pepple – Editor, *Able Muse*, 467 Saratoga Avenue #602, San Jose, CA 95129 USA

129

Corporeality

~ Stories by Hollis Seamon ~

978-1-927409-03-9 | Paperback

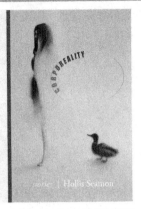

- **Gold Medal winner, 2014 Independent Book Publisher Outstanding Book Award**
- **Finalist, 2013 Foreword Review's Best Book of the Year**

"Seamon offers enough thematic and narrative variation to keep each story in this collection fresh." — *Publishers Weekly*

Sailing to Babylon

~ poems by **James Pollock** ~

978-0-9865338-7-7 | Paperback

- **Winner, Outstanding Achievement Award in Poetry from the Wisconsin Library Association**
- **Finalist, 2013 Griffin Poetry Prize**
- **Finalist, 2012 Governor General's Literary Award in Poetry**
- **Honorable Mention, 2012 Posner Poetry Book Award**

"A rich and complex array of subjects and allusions to provide both pleasure and challenge" — *Pleiades: A Journal of New Writing*

Strange Borderlands

~ Poems by Ben Berman ~

978-1-927409-05-3 | Paperback

- **Winner, 2014 Peace Corps Writers Best Book Award**
- **Finalist, 2014 Massachusetts Book Award**

"This is a must-have book for readers of poetry."
  — *Publishers Weekly,* starred review

Life in the Second Circle

~ Poems by Michael Cantor ~

978-0-9878705-5-1 | Paperback

- **Finalist, 2013 Massachusetts Book Award**

"A sensory kaleidoscope where the poems are more like movies."
  — Deborah Warren

ABLE MUSE PRESS // www.ablemusepress.com

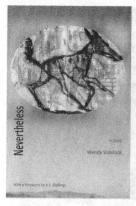

Nevertheless
~ Poems by Wendy Videlock ~
978-0-9865338-4-6 | Paperback

- **Finalist, 2012 Colorado Book Award**

"Videlock is a magician of play and pleasures, wisdom being not the least of these." — A.E. Stallings

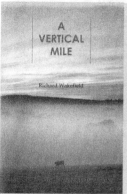

A Vertical Mile
~ Poems by Richard Wakefield ~
978-0-9878705-7-5 | Paperback

- **Shortlisted, 2014 Poets Prize**

"Wakefield crafts his verse to exacting standards yet keeps it uncontrived." — David Sanders

The Cosmic Purr
~ Poems by Aaron Poochigian ~
978-0-9878705-2-0 | Paperback

- **Shortlisted, 2014 Poets Prize**

"Aaron Poochigian's technique is masterly . . . and it's easy to be beguiled by these poems' wit and bravura. But the pyrotechnics are used to serious ends." — Dick Davis

Lines of Flight
~ Poems by Catherine Chandler ~
978-0-9865338-3-9 | Paperback

- **Shortlisted, 2013 Poets Prize**

"Lines of Flight is altogether a lively performance." — Richard Wilbur

Able Muse Anthology

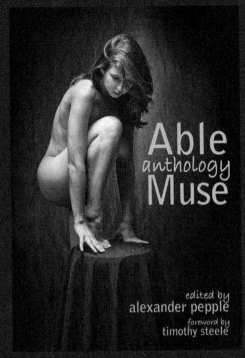

Edited by Alexander Pepple
Foreword by Timothy Steele
978-0-9865338-0-8 | Paperback

With R.S. Gwynn, Rhina P. Espaillat, Rachel Hadas, Mark Jarman, Timothy Murphy, Dick Davis, A.E. Stallings, Alan Sullivan, Deborah Warren, Diane Thiel, Leslie Monsour, Kevin Durkin, Turner Cassity, Kim Bridgford, Richard Moore and others.

. . . Here's a generous serving of the cream of Able Muse including not only formal verse but nonmetrical work that also displays careful craft, memorable fiction (seven remarkable stories), striking artwork and photography, and incisive prose. — X.J. Kennedy

Able Muse
Print Edition, No. 17
Summer 2014

TRANSLATION ANTHOLOGY FEATURE ISSUE
guest-edited by **Charles Martin**
978-1927409-45-9 | Paperback

WITH NEW TRANSLATIONS BY
X.J. Kennedy, Dick Davis, Julie Kane, Willis Barnstone, Tony Barnstone, William Baer, A.E. Stallings, Rachel Hadas, N.S. Thompson, Michael Palma, John Ridland, Jay Hopler, and others . . .

WITH NEW TRANSLATIONS OF
Victor Hugo, Arthur Rimbaud, C.P. Cavafy, Catullus, Charles Baudelaire, Francesco Petrarch, Rainer Maria Rilke, Asadullah Khan Ghalib, Horace, Martial, Heinrich Heine, Gaspara Stampa, Dante Alighieri, François Villon, Euripides, Georg Trakl, Paul Valéry, Christine de Pizan, and others . . .

TRANSLATION NOTES

তুমি কোন্ দলে

বাসের হাতল কেউ দ্রুত পায়ে ছুঁতে এলে আগে তাকে প্রশ্ন করো তুমি কোন্ দলে
ভুখা মুখে ভরা গ্রাস তুলে ধরবার আগে প্রশ্ন করো তুমি কোন্ দলে
পুলিশের গুলিতে যে পাথরে লুটোয় তাকে টেনে তুলবার আগে জেনে নাও দল
তোমার দুহাতে মাখা রক্ত কিন্তু বলো এর কোন্ হাতে রং আছে কোন্ হাতে নেই
টানলে মশালহাতে একে ওকে তাকে দেখো কার মুখে উলকি আছে কার মুখে নেই
কী কাজ কী কথা সেটা তত বড়ো কথা নয় আগে বলো তুমি কোন্ দল
কে মরেছে ভিলাইতে ছত্রিশগড়ের গাঁয়ে কে ছুটেছে কার মাথা নয় তত দামি
ঝন্ঝন্ নাচ হবে কোন্ পথে কোন্ পথ হতে পারে আরো লঘুগামী
বিচার দেবার আগে জেনে নাও দেগে দাও প্রশ্ন করো তুমি কোন্ দল
আত্মঘাতী ফাঁস থেকে বাসি শব খুলে এনে কানে কানে প্রশ্ন করো তুমি কোন্ দল
রাতে ঘুমোবার আগে ভালবাসবার আগে প্রশ্ন করো কোন্ দল তুমি কোন্ দল

— *Sankha Ghosh*
(Original Bengali poem)

133

"Tu te moques, jeune ribaude"

Tu te moques, jeune ribaude :
Si j'avais la tête aussi chaude
Que tu es chaude sous ta cotte,
Je n'aurais besoin de calotte,
Non plus qu'à ton ventre il ne faut
De pelisson, tant il est chaud.

Tous les charbons ardents
Allument là-dedans
Le plus chaud de leur braise ;
Un feu couvert en sort,
Plus fumeux et plus fort
Que l'air d'une fournaise.

J'ai la tête froide et gelée,
D'avoir ma cervelle écoulée
A ce limonier, par l'espace
De quatre ans, sans m'en savoir grâce,
Et lui voulant vaincre le cul,
Moi-même je me suis vaincu.

Ainsi, le fol sapeur
Au fondement trompeur
D'un Boulevard s'arrête,
Quand le faix, tout soudain
Ebranlé de sa main,
Lui écrase la tête.

— *Pierre de Ronsard*
  (Original French poem)

"Schattenküsse, Schattenliebe"

Schattenküsse, Schattenliebe,
Schattenleben, wunderbar!
Glaubst du, Närrin, alles bliebe
Unverändert, ewig wahr?

Was wir lieblich fest besessen,
Schwindet hin, wie Träumerein,
Und die Herzen, die vergessen,
Und die Augen schlafen ein.

— Heinrich Heine
(Original German poem)

Pumpkin Chucking
poems by Stephen Scaer
978-1-927409-12-1 | 2014 (Finalist, 2012 Able Muse Book Award)
". . . the poems are exquisitely lyrical . . . a wit that's wicked but not mean. He speaks for us all." — Deborah Warren

House Music
poems by Ellen Kaufman
978-1-927409-25-1 | 2014 (Finalist, 2012 Able Muse Book Award)
"Ellen Kaufman's poems . . . are astonishing acts of balance, intelligence, precision, eloquence, vision, imagination, and grace." — Vijay Seshadri

Heaven from Steam
poems by Carol Light
978-1-927409-18-3 | 2014 (Finalist, 2012 Able Muse Book Award)
"The overall effect is playful. . . . But she strikes another tone . . . the nimbleness with which she weaves and unweaves her lines and imagery." —Brad Leithauser

Credo for the Checkout Line in Winter
poems by Maryann Corbett
978-1-927409-14-5 | 2013 (Finalist, 2011 Able Muse Book Award)
"She is a newborn Robert Frost, with a wicked eye for contemporary life."
  —Willis Barnstone

Sea Level Rising
poems by John Philip Drury
978-1-927409-42-8 | 2015
". . . the 'film of beauty, tides that keep on rising' . . . *Sea Level Rising* is an amazing achievement. It should not be missed." — Erica Dawson

This Bed Our Bodies Shaped
poems by April Lindner
978-0-9878705-9-9 | 2012 (Finalist, 2011 Able Muse Book Award)
"The craft of these beautifully made verses is both seamless and palpable."
  — Mark Jarman

Compositions of the Dead Playing Flutes
poems by Barbara Ellen Sorensen
978-1-927409-23-7 | 2013
"These poems are attentive, scrupulous, and transforming, as they range from the sensuous to the spiritual." — Veronica Patterson

Asperity Street
poems by Gail White

978-1-927409-54-1 | 2015 (Special Honoree, 2014 Able Muse Book Award)

"... one of America's wittiest, most technically adept, funniest and most serious commentators on what it feels like to be human." — Rhina P. Espaillat

Slingshots and Love Plums
poems by Wendy Videlock

978-1-927409-52-7 | 2015

"The pleasures include off-kilter rhymes, elegant turns, earthy revelations, and the skillful mockery of pretentiousness in its various forms." — David Caplan

The Dark Gnu and Other Poems
written and illustrated by Wendy Videlock

978-1-927409-09-1 (pbk.) | 978-1-927409-13-8 (hc.) | 2013

"I found myself laughing and gasping in equal measures ... Videlock is so damn good and I'm so damn jealous of her talent." —Sherman Alexie

Uncontested Grounds
poems by William Conelly

978-1-927409-39-8 | 2015 (Finalist, 2013 Able Muse Book Award)

"Uncontested Grounds will stand as a notable book in this or any year." —X.J. Kennedy

Greed: A Confession
poems by D.R. Goodman

978-1-927409-38-1 | 2014 (Finalist, 2013 Able Muse Book Award)

"This poet is alive to everything. You want this book. It's terrific." —Kelly Cherry

Vellum
poems by Chelsea Woodard

978-1-927409-35-0 | 2014 (Finalist, 2013 Able Muse Book Award)

"In addition to her emotional maturity ... what makes these poems memorable is Woodard's obvious mastery of language, her flawless sentences." — Claudia Emerson

All the Wasted Beauty of the World
poems by Richard Newman

978-1-927409-31-2 | 2014 (Finalist, 2012 Able Muse Book Award)

"All the Wasted Beauty ... [puts] on the brakes and asking us to look, if only briefly, beyond our rear-views." — Dorianne Laux

Times Square and Other Stories
by William Baer
978-1-927409-43-5 | Paperback

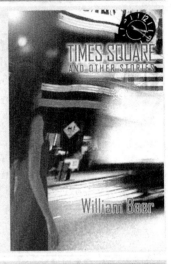

"Baer's twice-measured fictions, channel the reflecting reflections of James and Borges. . . . These fictions resuscitate Poe's unities of effects, breathing life back into the simulacrum of life. I loved this book!"

—Michael Martone

Taking Shape
Carmina Figurata
by Jan D. Hodge
ISBN 978-1-927409-56-5 (pbk.); 978-1-927409-58-9 (hc.)

"Jan D. Hodge is the master par excellence of *carmina figurata* . . . Hodge knows of grace, his poems are full of grace, and *Taking Shape,* like grace itself, is a gift of utter beauty."

— Vince Gotera

Grasshopper:
The Poetry of M A Griffiths
~ Now reprinted & distributed in the USA & Canada by **Able Muse Press**
978-1-904852-28-5 | Paperback

Margaret Ann Griffiths (1947-2009)

Grasshopper

The Poetry of
M A Griffiths

Margaret was born and raised in London and lived for some time in Bracknell then later moved to Poole. Rather than seek publication through traditional channels, she was content to share her work with fellow poets on various Internet forum. . . . In 2008, her "Opening a Jar of Dead Sea Mud" won *Eratosphere*'s annual Sonnet Bake-off, and was praised by Richard Wilbur. She was a Guest Poet on the Academy of American Poets website, where she was hailed as "one of the up-and-coming poets of our time."

She suffered for years from a stomach ailment which eventually proved fatal in July 2009. Almost immediately after her death was announced on *Eratosphere*, poets from all over the English-speaking world, from London, Derby, Scotland, Wales, Queensland, New South Wales, Massachusetts, New York, Minnesota, Missouri, Maryland, California and Texas collected her work for this publication.

CONTRIBUTOR NOTES

BRUCE BENNETT is the author of nine volumes of poetry and more than twenty-five poetry chapbooks. His most recent book is *Subway Figure* (Orchises Press, 2009), and his most recent chapbooks are *The Wither'd Sedge* (Finishing Line, 2014) and *Swimming in a Watering Can* (FootHills Publishing, 2014). In 2012 he was awarded a Pushcart Prize for a villanelle, "The Thing's Impossible," published in *Ploughshares*. In 2014 he retired from Wells College, where he had taught English and Creative Writing and directed the college's Visiting Writers Series since 1973. He was recently selected as the first recipient of the annual Writing the Rockies Lifetime Achievement Award for Excellence in the Teaching of Creative Writing.

ANDY BIGGS—See page 55.

CATHARINE SAVAGE BROSMAN is Professor Emerita of French at Tulane University. She was Mellon Professor of Humanities for 1990 and later held the Gore Chair in French. She was also visiting professor for a term at the University of Sheffield. Her scholarly publications comprise eighteen volumes on French literary history and criticism and two on American literature: *Louisiana Creole Literature: A Historical Study* (2013) and *Five Women Authors of the American Southwest: The Morality of Vision* (in press). She has published ten collections of verse, of which the latest is *On the Old Plaza* (2014), and two collections of personal essays. A third volume, *Music from the Lake and Other Essays,* is in press.

TERRI BROWN-DAVIDSON's first book of poetry, *The Carrington Monolgues* (Lit Pot Press), was nominated for the Pulitzer Prize in 2002. Her first novel, *Marie, Marie: Hold on Tight* (Lit Pot Press), was discussed in the *Writer* and published to excellent reviews. Terri is a fiction writer, poet, visual artist, and photographer who has received the Dillman Resort Scholarship for Colored Pencil, had her paintings featured in the group show Elementique, and won three Fresh Idea awards from the photography site 1x.com. Among other honors, she's received the AWP Intro Award in poetry, the New Mexico Writers fiction scholarship, and a Yaddo residency. Her poetry was featured in the anthology *Triquarterly New Writers.*

TERESE COE's poems and translations have appeared in *Able Muse, Alaska Quarterly Review,* the *Cincinnati Review, New American Writing, Ploughshares, Poetry, Threepenny Review, Agenda,* the

Moth, New Walk, New Writing Scotland, Poetry Review, the *TLS,* the *Stinging Fly,* and many other publications and anthologies. Her poem "More" was heli-dropped across London in the 2012 London Olympics Rain of Poems, and her latest collection of poems, *Shot Silk,* was published by Kelsay Books. She has a play in circulation, *Harry Smith at the Chelsea Hotel,* a biographical black comedy.

ANI DASGUPTA was born in Kolkata, India, and holds a PhD in Economics from Princeton University. He is a Professor at the Massachusetts Maritime Academy and the director of MMA's International Maritime Business Center. He has taught at Penn State, Tufts, and Boston Universities, in addition to serving as the chief economist of a dot-com and being a business consultant and software creator. He is currently working on a book-length project of "trans-creating" several of Sankha Ghosh's poems.

Born in 1981 near Washington, DC, JOHN ELLIS is a writer, editor, and teacher. He has lived, traveled, or studied throughout Western Europe, West Africa, and across the United States and served in the US military. He teaches English Literature in a private school in San Francisco and is a contributing writer and editor for a Northern California nonprofit that serves veterans. Currently, Ellis is a graduate student and teaching fellow in the Master of Fine Arts Program at Saint Mary's College of California, where he is writing his first book-length work, a memoir. He lives in San Francisco with his wife, Michelle.

JEANNE EMMONS has published three books of poetry: *Rootbound* (New Rivers Press), *Baseball Nights and DDT* (Pecan Grove Press), and *The Glove of the World* (Backwaters Press). She has won the Minnesota Voices Competition, the Backwaters Press Reader's Choice Award, the Comstock Poetry Award, the James Hearst Poetry Award, and the Sow's Ear Poetry Award, among others. Her work has appeared in *Alaska Quarterly,* the *American Scholar, Carolina Quarterly, Connecticut Review, South Carolina Review, North American Review, Poet Lore, Prairie Schooner, River Styx, South Dakota Review,* and many other journals. She is poetry editor of the *Briar Cliff Review.*

MIDGE GOLDBERG received the 2015 Richard Wilbur Poetry Award for her book *Snowman's Code,* and was a finalist for the 2015 Howard Nemerov Sonnet Award. Her poems have appeared in *Measure, Light, Raintown Review, Appalachia,* and on Garrison Keillor's a *Writer's Almanac.* Her poems are included in several anthologies, including *Rhyming Poems* and *Hot Sonnets.* Her other books include *Flume Ride* (2006) and the children's book *My Best Ever Grandpa* (2015). She is a longtime member of the Powow River Poets and has an MFA from the University of New Hampshire. She lives in Chester, New Hampshire, with her family, two cats, and an ever-changing number of chickens.

SANKHA GHOSH is widely considered the preeminent poet writing today in Bengali, a language spoken by more than 200 million people. Ghosh was born in Chandpur, Bangladesh in 1932, and currently resides in Kolkata, India. His first book of poems came out in 1956 and he is the author of more than two dozen volumes of poetry and several volumes of literary criticisms. His poetry is renowned for its aural splendor, density of images, and an acerbic tone often directed at perpetrators of social and political malfeasances. Among his numerous awards are the Shahityo Academy Award, the highest award given by the Indian Academy of Letters, and the Padma Bibhushan, a civilian award conferred by the Government of India.

BARBARA HAAS has published prose in *Glimmer Train, Western Humanities Review,* and the *Georgia Review.* She is a repeat contributor to the *Hudson Review, Virginia Quarterly Review,* and the *North American Review.* She has nonfiction forthcoming from the *Chariton Review,* the *MacGuffin,* and *Sinister Wisdom.*

The latest of RACHEL HADAS's many books of poetry is *Questions in the Vestibule* (Northwestern University Press, April 2016). She is currently at work on verse translations of Euripides' two *Iphigenia* plays, also for Northwestern. Rachel is Board of Governors Professor of English at Rutgers University-Newark. Of "Brunch at Bed & Ink," Rachel writes:

"Ken Arnold was Director of Rutgers University Press in the early 1990s. It is thanks to Ken that my books *Living in Time, Mirrors of Astonishment,* and *Other Worlds Than This* were published—essays, poetry, and translations respectively, none of them money-makers, none calculated to promote Ken's career. After Ken left Rutgers University Press, we lost touch, but in 2012 life brought us together again. Ken was now living in Portland, Oregon—living and dying of prostate cancer.

"My son was also in Portland. I last saw Ken around Thanksgiving 2013, when he and his beloved Carol and I and my beloved Shalom shared a memorable brunch with my son at a sunny place on Hawthorne. The talk was of Buddhism, Japan, poetry, travel, and the miracle of love late in life.

"Ever tranquil and courageous and curious, Ken Arnold died in January 2014."

HEINRICH HEINE was born in Düsseldorf, Germany, in either 1797 or 1799. In 1831 he took exile in France, where he often struggled financially despite irregular patronage from a millionaire uncle. With freedom of speech he developed an international reputation for the lyricism, wordplay, irony, and excoriating satire of his poems, and was called the last of the Romantics. In 1841 he married Crescence Eugénie Mirat ("Mathilde"), who cared for him during eight years of paralysis; he wrote from bed until his death in 1856. His books would eventually be burned by the Nazis, creating prophecy out of his statement, "Where they have burned books, they will end in burning human beings." His tomb is in Montmartre Cemetery in Paris.

JOSEPH HUTCHISON, currently serving as Poet Laureate of Colorado, is the author of sixteen collections of poems, including *The Satire Lounge, Marked Men, Thread of the Real,* and *Bed of Coals.* He has also coedited, with Andrea Watson, the FutureCycle Press Good Works anthology *Malala: Poems for Malala Yousafzai* (all profits to the Malala Foundation). In Fall 2016 the book publishing arm of the New York Quarterly Foundation, NYQ Books, will issue his collection *The World as Is: New & Selected Poems 1972–2015.* He teaches in and directs the Arts & Culture program for the University of Denver's University College and lives with his wife, Iyengar yoga instructor Melody Madonna, in the mountains southwest of Denver.

AMANDA JERNIGAN—See page 99.

JEAN L. KREILING's first collection of poems, *The Truth in Dissonance* (Kelsay Books), was published in 2014. Her work has appeared widely in print and online journals, including *American Arts Quarterly, Angle,* the *Evansville Review, Measure,* and *Mezzo Cammin,* and in several anthologies. Kreiling is a past winner of the String Poet Prize and the Able Muse Write Prize, and she has been a finalist for the Frost Farm Prize, the Howard Nemerov Sonnet Award, and the Richard Wilbur Poetry Award.

AMIT MAJMUDAR is a widely published poet, novelist, and essayist. He is also a diagnostic nuclear radiologist and the state of Ohio's first Poet Laureate. His latest book is *Dothead* (Alfred A. Knopf, March 2016).

RON MCFARLAND teaches creative writing and literature at the University of Idaho. His most recent book is a biography of Lieutenant Colonel Edward J. Steptoe (1815–1865) entitled *Edward J. Steptoe and the Indian Wars* (2016). His book, *Appropriating Hemingway* (2014), concerns Ernest Hemingway's appearance as a character in popular fiction and other genres.

ANGE MLINKO is the author of four books of poetry, including *Marvelous Things Overheard, Shoulder Season,* which was a finalist for the William Carlos Williams Award, and *Starred Wire,* a National Poetry Series pick and finalist for the James Laughlin Award. She has been the recipient of a Guggenheim Fellowship and the Randall Jarrell Award for Criticism, and served as poetry editor for the *Nation.* Her essays and reviews have been published in *The Nation, The London Review of Books, Poetry,* and *Parnassus.* Educated at St. John's College and Brown University, she has lived abroad in Morocco and Lebanon, and is currently Associate Professor of English at the University of Florida. She lives in Gainesville.

JOHN CHRISTOPHER NELSON was raised between ninety-four acres of chaparral in San Diego County and a defunct mining town in the Nevada high desert. He earned his BA in American Literature from UCLA, where he was executive editor of *Westwind.* John is a graduate of the Stonecoast MFA in Creative Writing, where he has served a variety of roles—including editor-in-chief—on the *Stonecoast Review.* John has work forthcoming in *Indicia* and *Chiron Review,* and is published in *Stone House: A Literary Anthology.* His writing was included in *It's All Been Done before but Not by Me,* an installation through the Hammer Museum. He currently lives in Seattle.

STEPHEN PALOS is from Lexington, KY. He received his BA in English from the Ohio State University and his MFA in creative writing from the University of Michigan, where he won a Hopwood Graduate Poetry Award and was awarded a Zell Fellowship for 2015–2016. His work has appeared in the *Allegheny Review* and *Pluck! Journal* and is forthcoming in the *Raintown Review.* He was the 2013 winner of the Iris N. Spencer Poetry Award and has been awarded fellowships to attend The Twenty: A Kentucky Young Writers Advance and The Bucknell Seminar for Younger Poets. In his spare time, Stephen writes and illustrates riddle poems.

PIERRE DE RONSARD (1524–1585) was attached to both the French and Scottish courts in his youth; he was later named royal poet for the House of Valois. He led the group of poets called the Pleiades, who looked to classical poetry for paradigms but wrote in French rather than Latin to encourage the development of French literature. In *An Introduction to the French Poets,* Geoffrey Brereton writes, "He projected . . . an image of his own century. . . . It was precisely Ronsard's inability to either assimilate his models or to forget them which gave his work its character."

A mathematician by profession, PEDRO POITEVIN is a bilingual poet and translator originally from Guatemala. He is a contributor to *Letras Libres* and *Periódico de Poesía,* the poetry journal of the National Autonomous University of Mexico (UNAM). Poems in English have appeared or are forthcoming in *Rattle, River Styx, Cossack Review, Angle, Think,* and *Nashville Review,* among other venues.

TIMOTHY MURPHY hunts and farmed in the Dakotas. A double volume of his poems, *Mortal Stakes* and *Faint Thunder,* was published in August 2011 by the Lewis and Clark Foundation's Dakota Institute Press. His first selected poems, albeit on a single theme, *Hunter's Log: Field Notes 1988–2011,* was released under the same imprint in November 2011. A second selected, *Devotions,* is forthcoming from the North Dakota State University Press in January 2017.

TIMOTHY REILLY was a professional tuba player in both the United States and Europe during the 1970s (in 1978, he was a member of the orchestra of the Teatro Regio in Turin, Italy). He is currently a retired substitute teacher, living in Southern California with his wife, Jo-Anne Cappeluti, a published poet and scholar. He has published widely, most recently in *Superstition Review, Grey Sparrow, Florida English,* and *Relief.* His stories have also appeared in *Slow Trains Literary Journal, Amarillo Bay,* and *Seattle Review,* as well as other print and online journals.

N.S. THOMPSON lives near Oxford, UK. His most recent book of poetry is *Letter to Auden* (Smokestack, 2010), a verse epistle in rime royal. He is the coeditor with Andy Croft of *A Modern Don Juan: Cantos for These Times by Divers Hands* (Five Leaves, 2014), a collection of new verse narratives bringing Byron's hero into the modern world. His collection, *Line Dancing,* is forthcoming from Red Squirrel and a collection of his translations of Pier Paolo Pasolini, *The Ashes of Gramsci,* is also planned. He reviews widely and is a nonfiction editor for *Able Muse.*

ANDREW VALENTINE's stories have appeared in *Literary Orphans, Chagrin River Review, Pioneertown, Poplorish!* and the *Shrug,* among others. He lives and writes in Eugene, OR.

DORIS WATTS lives in Temecula, California. She is a graduate of the University of Redlands and of San Diego State University, where she completed a special major master's degree in technical communication. Her work has appeared in the *Formalist, Mezzo Cammin, 14x14, Blue Unicorn,* the *Lyric,* and *Autumn Sky Daily.*

ABLE MUSE BOOK AWARD WINNERS

Cause for Concern
~ Poems by Carrie Shipers ~
WINNER - 2014 ABLE MUSE BOOK AWARD SELECTED BY MOLLY PEACOCK

978-1-927409-59-6 | Paperback

"Her poet's craft, palpable in every arresting line, makes the subtlest turns of vulnerability with enviable poise." — Molly Peacock

". . . such exquisite, irresistible and terrifying honesty." — Kwame Dawes

Walking in on People
~ poems by Melissa Balmain ~
WINNER - 2013 ABLE MUSE BOOK AWARD, SELECTED BY X.J. KENNEDY

978-1-927409-29-9 | Paperback

"Melissa Balmain's poems add to the rhythmic bounce of light verse a darker, more cutting humor. The result is an infectious, often hilarious blend of the sweet and the lethal, the charming and the acidic."
— Billy Collins

Virtue, Big as Sin
~ poems by Frank Osen ~
WINNER - 2012 ABLE MUSE BOOK AWARD, selected by MARY JO SALTER

978-1-927409-16-9 | Paperback

"In his talent for tragedy and comedy, and for mixing them, Osen takes his place in a distinguished line of English-language poets that runs from Chaucer and Shakespeare down to our day."
—Timothy Steele (from the afterword)

Dirge for an Imaginary World
~ poems by Matthew Buckley Smith ~
WINNER - 2011 ABLE MUSE BOOK AWARD, selected by ANDREW HUDGINS

978-0-9878705-0-6 | Paperback

"The range of subjects is equally and as charmingly eclectic . . . Mental and linguistic agility generously challenge the reader in poem after poem."
— Greg Williamson (from the foreword)

Details at www.AbleMusePress.com

INDEX

INDEX

Able Muse – No. 16, Winter 2013
Jehanne Dubrow, featured poet | **Peter Svensson**, featured artist
978-1-927409-27-5

- with rachel hadas, marly youmans, r.s. gwynn, cheryl diane kidder, a.e. stallings, david mason, chrissy mason, peter byrne, rory waterman, and others

Able Muse – No. 15, Summer 2013
Greg Williamson, featured poet | **Clara Lieu**, featured artist
978-1-927409-21-3

- with dick allen, fred longworth, robert j. levy, haley hach, jonathan danielson, david mason, peter byrne, david caplan, stephen kampa, n.s. thompson, and others

Able Muse – No. 14, Winter 2012
Catherine Tufariello, featured poet | **Nicolas Evariste**, featured artist
978-1-927409-07-7

- with thomas carper, lorna knowles blake, richard wakefield, tony barnstone, len krisak, evelyn somers, gregory dowling, aaron poochigian, and others

Able Muse – No. 13, Summer 2012
Patricia Smith, featured poet | **Andrew Ponomarenko**, featured artist
978-1-927409-01-5

- with wendy videlock, jennifer reeser, richard wakefield, julie bruck, kim bridgford, brian culhane, reginald dwayne betts, and others

Able Muse – No.12, Winter 2011
David Mason, featured poet | **Alper Çukur**, featured artist
978-0-9865338-9-1

- with suzanne j. doyle, timothy murphy, gabriel spera, richard wakefield, lyn lifshin, amit majmudar, rachel bentley, david j. rothman, and others

Able Muse – No. 11, Summer 2011
Catharine Savage Brosman, featured poet | **Emily Leonne Bennett**, featured artist
978-0-9865338-5-3

- with david mason, andrew waterman, john drury, rachel hadas, brian culhane, emily laithauser, leslie monsour, traci chee, and other

Able Muse – No. 10, Inaugural Print Edition, Winter 2010
R.P. Lister, featured poet | **Massimo Sbrini**, featured artist
978-0-9865338-2-2

- with catherine tufariello, catharine savage brosman, leslie monsour, j. patrick lewis, kim bridgford, nancy lou canyon, john whitworth, peter filkins, and others

CPSIA information can be obtained
at www.ICGtesting.com
Printed in the USA
LVOW03s0849220716

497350LV00002B/4/P